Dana Manciagli's book is very important es
economic recovery. She is preparing peopl

Stedman Graham,
Author, Speaker, Entrepreneur

Dana tackles all important elements and **Cut the Crap, Get a Job!** *is a great resource for anyone looking to take the next step in their career. In the book, you'll learn ways to manage the emotional stress of looking for work, some killer organizational tools to keep you on track, some tips around social media, interview skills and follow-up. If I were looking for work, I'd have a dog eared copy on my desk, highlighted and underlined. Excellent resource!*

—Joshua Waldman,
author of *Job Searching with Social Media For Dummies*
and *The Social Media Job Search Workbook*

Welcome to the new reality! **Cut the Crap, Get a Job!** *is a welcome slap in the face to conventional job search "wisdom". Dana shows you how to embrace your talents, understand your talents and land a job you'll like. I highly recommend you invest the time in yourself to read it – because you're worth it.*

—David Perry,
co-author of *Guerrilla Marketing for Job Hunters 3.0*
and Managing Partner of Perry-Martel International Inc.

Dana Manciagli has created a candid, comprehensive guide to landing the right job the right way. **Cut the Crap, Get a Job!** *is a goldmine of innovative strategies and practical advice, backed by solid research. A brilliant and generous gift to job-seekers everywhere, from college students to senior executives!*

—Ford R. Myers,
President of Career Potential, LLC
and author of *Get The Job You Want, Even When No One's Hiring*

Dana Manciagli's book on job search is concise, practical and ground-breaking. Her no-nonsense approach elevates the job search game to a whole new level. She methodically provides a fresh and perceptive insight that changes the rules of traditional job hunting techniques. Her book is an extremely valuable tool in today's competitive job market where new tools need to be used to accelerate job offers.

—Joe Carroll, SPHR, CMF,
Author of *How To Get a Great Job in 90 Days or Less*

"Dana talks straight and lays out what you need to know to effectively manage a modern job search. Make no mistake, today's career transition requires a different set of skills and tools. If you want to acquire them, you need this book!"

—Bud Clarkson,
author of *Job Search Strategies: Get a Good Job Even in a Bad Economy*

"*Dana Manciagli, having led a remarkable career, tells the reader like it is to* **Cut the Crap, Get a Job**! *As a mentor, her logical step-by-step approach, including the latest techniques of 'social recruiting,' will indeed focus you in the right direction to achieve powerful results.*"

—Susan Bulkeley Butler,
CEO of the Susan Bulkeley Butler Institute for the Development of Women Leaders, former managing partner at Accenture, and author of *Become the CEO of You, Inc.* and *Women Count: A Guide to Changing the World*

"*Dana is the master motivator who has been there and done that. She is going to tell you the way things are, but caringly awaken the winner in you. If you are ready to stop complaining and make a move, this book can change your life. I can assure you that you will leave with a game plan to get that dream job.*"

—Sandeep Krishnamurthy, Ph.D.
and director of the University of Washington Bothell School of Business

"*Job seekers would be well advised to heed Dana's advice. A clear focus on activities that bring results—such as modern day networking techniques—is critical in today's job market. Dana will help you cut through the hype and focus on doing those things most likely to bring job search success. Highly recommended.*"

—Tony Restell,
director and co-founder of Top-Consultant.com and Social-Hire.com

"*Dana's new book is brimming with invaluable 'how-to' guidance for anyone navigating their career in the turbulent job market today. Not only does she tell you want to do, she shows you how to stay confident, resilient, and optimistic in the process. This is a don't miss read!*"

—Kathy Cramer, Ph.D.,
managing partner of the Cramer Institute, and author of *Change the Way You See Everything Through Asset-Based Thinking*

"*Dana Manciagli has developed a clear process that challenges job seekers to take control of their job searches. Each chapter includes specific job search mistakes and excuses to avoid as well as tricks and solutions to use, which enable readers to put what they learn into action immediately.* **Cut the Crap, Get a Job**! *is a resource that all committed job seekers should have in their hands.*"

—Susan Gunelius,
president and CEO of KeySplash Creative, Inc.,
founder of WomenOnBusiness.com, and author of 10 business books

"*Dana nails it! Helping job seekers understand the importance of the written word is golden! This is a must-read for anyone seeking a position.*"

—Dr. Julie Miller,
president and author of *Business Writing That Counts!*

"**Cut the Crap, Get a Job!** provides the two essentials you must have to get a job in the 21st century: the right attitude and the right tactics. Dana's 'nothing can stop me,' hyper-positive, can-do attitude oozes out of this book. If you can harness that attitude and be disciplined enough to follow her simple instructions, there is no doubt: you will win a job!"

—Ilise Benun,
author of 7 books and founder of Marketing-Mentor.com
and the Creative Freelancer Conference

"A direct, no-nonsense tool to help you get out of 'overwhelm' and into action to get the job you want NOW!"

—Anna Liotta,
author of *Unlocking Generational CODES*

"Dana Manciagli has advice every job seeker needs to hear. And she delivers it in user-friendly, easy-to-digest fashion. Her newest book, **Cut the Crap, Get a Job!** has what the unemployed need to hear. Replete with bulleted lists, statistics, solutions, stories, steps, benefits, recent research, tools, tricks, charts, and homework assignments, Manciagli takes readers beyond the obvious. She leads them to improved views of themselves and their likely success. Along the way, she helps them avoid mistakes and encourages them not to make excuses. If finding a job is your most immediate goal, you need to read this book in order to achieve it."

—Dr. Marlene Caroselli,
keynoter, corporate trainer, and author of over 60 books, including *Hiring and Firing, The Critical Thinking Tool Kit,* and *Principled Persuasion,* named a Director's Choice by Doubleday Book Club.

CUT THE CRAP, GET A JOB!

A NEW JOB SEARCH PROCESS FOR A NEW ERA

"FOR THE SERIOUS JOB SEEKER, FROM COLLEGE GRADUATE TO SENIOR EXECUTIVE"

DANA MANCIAGLI

AUTHORITY
PUBLISHING

Cut the Crap, Get a Job! A New Job Search Process for a New Era

By Dana Manciagli

1. BUSINESS AND ECONOMICS / Careers / Job Hunting 2. BUSINESS AND ECONOMICS / Careers / General 3. BUSINESS AND ECONOMICS / Careers / Resumes

ISBN: 978-1-935953-47-0

Cover design by Lewis Agrell

Interior Design by Stephanie Martindale

Printed in the United States of America

Authority Publishing
11230 Gold Express Dr. #310-413
Gold River, CA 95670
800-877-1097
www.AuthorityPublishing.com

Microsoft® and Microsoft Excel® and Microsoft Word® and Microsoft OneNote® are registered trademarks of Microsoft Corporation. DanaManciagli.com is not associated with Microsoft.

THIS BOOK IS DEDICATED TO TWO AMAZING ORGANIZATIONS:

➢ **Junior Achievement (JA)** in 120 countries around the world. Junior Achievement teaches young people between the ages of 5 and 25 about money management and how business works. JA is equipping them with the skills they need to own their economic success. In summary, Junior Achievement inspires and prepares young people to succeed in a global economy.

Junior Achievement currently reaches over 10 million students globally, with 400,000 volunteers, and there is so much more demand than supply. I urge you to contact your local Junior Achievement (JA) office and offer your volunteer time or money.

A portion of this book's proceeds will be donated to Junior Achievement of Washington State.

➢ **The Military professionals** who have served our country and are now aspiring to enter the non-military workforce. They have such amazing skills, values, and drive, and we must embrace them in this new era of employment. Globally, not just the U.S.

CONTENTS

Acknowledgments   xi

Introduction   xiii

Section 1: Attitude, Commitment, and Goal-Setting   **1**

    Chapter 1: Get Ready to Compete—In Your Head   3

    Chapter 2: Commit to the Odds Game   13

    Chapter 3: Set a Goal before Applying for Jobs   19

    Chapter 4: Outline Your Job Search Plan   29

Section 2: Preparing to Win a Job   **35**

    Chapter 5: Build Your Job Tracking Tool   37

    Chapter 6: Sources for Jobs, Online and Offline   47

    Chapter 7: Social Media's Role in Job Search   55

    Chapter 8: Research, Research, Research   67

    Chapter 9: Interview Preparation—In Advance   73

    Chapter 10: Network for Jobs   83

    Chapter 11: Cold Calling Companies   101

Section 3: Apply, Interview, Follow Up   **109**

    Chapter 12: Phone Etiquette   111

    Chapter 13: Email Etiquette   121

    Chapter 14: Résumé Tips and Tricks   129

    Chapter 15: Applying for a Position   143

    Chapter 16: Cover Letter Overhaul   151

    Chapter 17: Winning Interviews to Win a Job   163

    Chapter 18: Thank You and Follow-Up   181

About the Author   187

ACKNOWLEDGMENTS

Thank you to thousands of job seekers, career coaches, and coworkers who have pushed me to write this book. I made the commitment about eight years ago and have been encouraged to "cut the crap" and document my expertise with millions via this book.

Thank you to my darling Mathis Dunn, who already thought I was crazy before this writing adventure. Now, he's just smiling with me through my journey and he's no longer numb to the clicking of my computer keyboard all day and night. He helps me laugh at myself, too, which is a wonderful thing.

Thanks to my mom, Ilse Metchek, who inspires me to do my best, try new things, and sit up straight while doing all of the above. My twin sister, or "womb-mate," Tracy Frank, has motivated me by showing me her strength battling breast cancer twice, raising an amazing son, Milo, and giving back to the world by training Parkinson's patients. My close friends and family have heard my dreams of writing for years, so thank you to them for believing (and waiting).

I couldn't write this section without acknowledging my two wonderful children, Shane and Chad. They have always inspired me to reach for the stars because they always showed interest, asked questions, and gave me advice (or rolled their eyes out of sheer embarrassment). As an example, Chad recommended I work for Microsoft after my start-up since he liked gaming on the XBOX... so I did. And Shane showed me an adventurous side by going to college in Boston, volunteering in the Dominican Republic, and pushing himself in extreme sports. Finally, I'm proud to say that both of my grown boys are armed with university degrees and are gainfully employed with Fortune 500 companies. Now I get to focus on doing what I said I would do: help people with their careers, networking, and job searches.

INTRODUCTION

Barbara Howell, a 35-year-old marketing director, is stuck. She feels frustrated, depressed, scared, and unmotivated. She has already spent three months sending multiple résumés to online job postings with no results and is losing confidence in her skills and abilities. These feelings prevent most qualified candidates from getting a job. Barbara needs to start over. She needs to turn off her job search engine and restart the car.

Bob Hillman, 50, and a successful finance vice president, is confident and very busy applying to multiple job postings. During his prior job searches, he would hear about jobs through buddies and get them almost every time. But this time, he has typos in his résumé, arrives just in time for interviews, does not do any research, and creates answers on the fly in his interviews. In summary, Bob has gotten lazy and sloppy and reliant on what used to work for him. As a result, he is not winning a job.

Barbara and Bob need to **Cut the Crap and Get a Job!** Crap comes in two forms: **excuses** and **mistakes**. Barbara needs to pick herself up, emotionally, get over her excuses, and change her approach. Bob needs to begin with a more disciplined process, fix his mistakes, and take his job search steps much more seriously. If both cut the crap, they will get a job.

If you haven't studied and practiced job search skills recently, you should assume you are terrible at job search. Here's why.

- The job market has changed tremendously, both the hiring process and the competition.

- Bosses and interviewers will notice the big and the little mistakes. Mistakes are signs that you might also make mistakes at the job you're applying for.

- Technology is used much more by hiring companies to recruit, screen, interview, and more. They also expect you to use technology professionally (documents, emails, etc.).

Only the best candidates win jobs. Yes, it is a competition, so I will use the word "winning" throughout this book. Plus, hiring managers want to hire someone who has the skills they need and someone who is going to be successful. However, the way most job seekers are hunting for jobs today is working against them. Two major barriers exist. One, preparation and applications are flawed. Two, if they get past the first barrier, they're making enough errors in the interview process to sabotage any chance they had.

This book will not only teach **you** how to win against both barriers, but it will give you new, innovative ways to stand out and get the job you want. You're going to stand out by being THE BEST, using new tools and application approaches, and by beating your competition. "Cut the Crap, Get a Job!" applies to all types of job seekers: employed-but-looking, unemployed, career-changers, re-entering the workforce, pre-graduation search, and more.

Warning: this book is not for the thin-skinned or those who want the easy way. I am often called *"The Suze Orman or Jillian Michaels of Careers."* My cut-the-crap approach is for the serious job seeker, and it won't be easy. My job process calls for discipline, attention to detail, and incredible organization. You will become a "job search engineer" and be relentlessly focused on every step you take. Any slip-up can be the reason you aren't winning a job.

What you will need before beginning:

1. An understanding of what kind of job(s) you are searching for. If you don't know, seek out great resources on this topic. This book picks up with the assumption you have a sense of what you want to do next. Be able to articulate at least 2-3 types of jobs you want. I'll help you set your job goal in the first section of this book and with the tools found at danamanciagli.com.

2. Access to a computer. If you don't have one, you can use a library, hourly rental facilities, schools, internet cafés, *or* make an investment in a refurbished or new PC (this can be a tax write-off). There are two reasons why you need one. One, to learn how to use computers as a skill for your job and, two, to manage your job search process information end-to-end.

3. Strong commitment to find the job you want as quickly as possible *and* a willingness to put the time into the process.

Tom Campbell is recently unemployed and doesn't even know where to start. During his career, he has never needed to search for a new job, either within his company or externally. He told me "jobs always came to me, either through friends or fellow employees."

Elizabeth Conroy conducted a job search process ten years ago and was very successful. But what she used to do is not working today. She is sending out résumés, posting on job boards, and applying to jobs. Nothing is working. Elizabeth needs to erase her outdated steps and start all over. She needs to take control and change her game.

Think back to when you learned how to drive, how to play a new sport, or how to use a computer. Many of you followed step-by-step instructions and learned what happened when you made mistakes. The only difference with your job search process is that the world has changed around you. So the instruction manual has changed.

Are you committed? Are you willing to restart your job search effort from step one? Are you open to changing virtually everything you have been doing and trying new approaches? The Cut the Crap job search process is not only a full-time job, it requires you to be the best with every step you take.

SECTION 1
ATTITUDE, COMMITMENT, AND GOAL-SETTING

DO NOT START APPLYING AT THIS STAGE

You think you're ready. You've got your résumé updated, and you're ready to start submitting. Some of you have searched for employment many times and others have never had to. Regardless of what type of job seeker you are, I have good news and bad news. The bad news first: The entire landscape of job searching has changed. It's a new era and you are not current. The good news: There are experts who want to see you win the job you want in this highly competitive market.

So, four words: **You are not ready**.

Start from zero, build a brand new job search program for yourself, and see the results.

CHAPTER 1
GET READY TO COMPETE—IN YOUR HEAD

Do you really want to get a job? Are you fully committed or just thinking about it? Is this important or just a hobby? With the right step-by-step instruction, combined with your full commitment, you **will** be successful.

First, you need to get your head screwed on straight. I'm not a psychologist, and, frankly, motivational "pep talks" did not help me when I hit the job search blues (multiple times). But having a bad attitude can hurt your efforts, and being positive will definitely help you.

#1 Challenge: Combatting negative feelings during your job search

"I became depressed. This was the sort of depression where I stopped talking to friends or family—I was in a black mood. My dream of becoming a marketing director was fading."

If you've never felt any of the following, you are not human: frustrated, depressed, angry, confused, guilty, sad, victimized, stupid, inept, humiliated, embarrassed, awkward, lacking confidence.

Searching for a job is hard. No, very hard. It triggers negative emotions, especially if you are unemployed. But the same holds true for those employed and searching within their own company or who need to make a move outside their company. Think about it. You are selling your skills to employers. They are the decision-makers, with multiple applicants to choose from. It is not clear exactly what the employers are looking for, if they are even looking at you, or why you are not "chosen." In school, the team captains picked their best players and nobody wanted to be the last person standing. Worse, in the job search world, only one gets "picked" and many others are not.

There is no transparency to what is going on during the hiring process, either. You don't know if your application or résumé is being looked at. And you will never know. Even if someone looks at your application, you will not know why you didn't get the interview. Then, you won't know why you didn't get the job. There are multiple inexplicable reasons why you didn't win a specific job, but here are some of the most probable:

- The job went to an internal candidate, someone already working for the company or already within that department.

- They hired another external candidate who had stronger skills.

- They are still looking since they didn't find anyone who met their criteria.

- They decided not to fill this job at this time. Or they changed the specification and reposted.

- Another candidate knew somebody who knew somebody who knew somebody...through networking (see Chapter 10, Network for Jobs).

Regardless if you are at the beginning, middle, or end of the job search process, know that it is not designed to make you feel good (or bad). However, please remember:

- Millions of people are searching right now, along with you.

- Many others are not being "picked" for a job today. You have company. But they are continuing to search tomorrow. Will you?

- You will never know who won the job or why...or why you didn't. Don't waste energy finding out or trying to figure it out on your own. Move on. This book will help expose errors you may have been making so you get a chance to correct them.

- Stop being the victim. *"I'm not hearing back"* or *"I'm waiting to hear something."* Hiring managers and human resources are not obligated to return your calls, respond to your application, or advise if you are in the running. Yes, they would like to and they do want you to have a positive perception of their company. However, they don't have time. Their job has one purpose: to identify and select the very best candidate for their job.

- Be humble. Yes, I know you believe you are perfect for that job you just read about. And you know you are the best in the world at what you do. However, no candidate is perfect. And no good hiring manager will believe you if you say you can do it all. Learn humility, show it early in the application process, and get excited about learning something new with every job.

SOLUTION: HERE ARE FIVE WAYS TO GET READY FOR YOUR JOB SEARCH PROCESS, MENTALLY AND EMOTIONALLY

1 READ MOTIVATIONAL BOOKS, ARTICLES, WEBSITES

One of my favorite books is *Change the Way You See Everything* by Kathryn D. Cramer, Ph.D. and Hank Wasiak. Not only is this book beautiful, but the advice helped me through cancer and a job search (separate times). Here are some of my favorite insights:

Deficit-Based Thinking		Asset-Based Thinking
I'll never make it...	➔	Put one foot in front of the other and move.
That's impossible	➔	What is possible?
I'll never get this done!	➔	This will take longer than I expected.
What's the matter with me?	➔	What am I learning?

Magnify What's Best and Focus on What's Next

(+) Set your sights on what you want/need.

(+) Move past fear.

(+) Set your sights on the next step.

Imitate Shamelessly and Often

The fastest way to learn anything is to imitate a role model...

For asset-based thinkers, acquiring new insights and skills by imitating the values, beliefs, approaches, and behaviors of individuals they admire is a way of life.

Invest time right now in figuring out where you are "stuck" and get "un-stuck" immediately. Whatever works for you, just do it.

2 PARTNER WITH A FRIEND, ANOTHER JOB SEEKER, A COACH... SOMEBODY

Friends can provide support, proof your writing, help you celebrate the steps on the journey, and give you new ideas. They can also show "tough love" by kicking you in the pants, scolding you for the excuses you will make up, and getting you motivated.

Other resources may be found online in job search forums and career websites where there are communities of others who are job seeking right now. See Chapter 6 for sources.

3 GIVE YOUR JOB SEARCH A PROJECT NAME—MAKE IT A "THING," AN ADVENTURE, A PROJECT

Think of some accomplishments you have made during your lifetime. It may have been "The Easter 5K," "Graduation," or "Had a Baby." Well, here is another accomplishment in development. So name it now. Call it "My Job Winning Project," "Job Search Mission," or "Fred." Place a huge label on this journey, which is another race. Because there *is* a finish line and you *will* be celebrating.

How many of you have managed projects at school or work? Completed a term paper, wrote a monthly report, balanced a budget, closed a sales order, or any other milestone in your life? This is no different. It has a start, an end, and all kinds of steps in the middle. The steps are not always clear, and the outcomes of each move are not what you anticipated.

4 TALK POSITIVELY TO AND ABOUT YOURSELF EVERY DAY

Sounds corny, I know. But it works. Keep reminding yourself:

- This is my chance to find the job I truly want and possibly make more money.

- I know there are jobs and that I can help hiring managers with their need to fill a role.

- I can convince them that I am the best hire for them, even in a crowded market.

- I am optimistic and excited to be in job-search mode, as I will learn and get better every day.

5 GET PROFESSIONAL HELP.

If you have been looking for a job for a long time without success, it's reasonable that you might feel down. But if you don't deal with the problem, you'll likely continue experiencing and feeling defeat.

Get some help from a counselor, a therapist, or another professional who can help you regain your perspective. You need to deal with this, along with any other toxic mindsets, to give yourself the best chance of landing the job you really want.

TRICKS

1 Smile when you talk about your "Job Search Project" or "Fred." You will be surprised how your own non-verbal actions can adjust your emotions.

2 Surround yourself with supportive people versus those who say, "Why do you want another job?" or "What's wrong with what you have?"

3 Start a collection of job search tips widely available on the web. Start at http://danamanciagli.com and hear other experts, too, referencing my "Resources" tab.

MISTAKES

Mistake #1: Spending time with other negative people. Just say no.

Mistake #2: Giving yourself another week to wallow. Wake up tomorrow to begin fresh. Catch yourself using the four-letter word that starts with a "W:" W-A-I-T. "I'm waiting to hear back," or "I'll wait until after the holidays." No more waiting.

Mistake #3: Drinking, drugs, not working out...letting your physical status deteriorate with your emotional state.

Mistake #4: Asking or letting someone else conduct your job search for you. Do not allow your spouse, girlfriend, parent, or other person apply on your behalf, write your cover letters for you, or organize your process. You need to be either fully accountable or stop looking. Use your friends and family as coaches, motivators, and support.

EXCUSES

Excuse #1: *"I don't know who to go to for support."* There is more than enough help for you in numerous places. Online, alumni support, career centers, outplacement firms, career coaches. My guess: You're not asking for support.

Excuse #2: *"I guess I'm not that good."* Really? Did you know there is a hiring manager *right now* who is losing sleep because he or she can't find a good candidate like you? There are jobs for everybody and you have skills. Learn how to identify and promote the right skills just ahead in this book.

Excuse #3: *"I don't have any role models."* Your role models can be experts available to help you at little to no cost right now. Online discussion boards, articles, and so much more. Beware of being too hung up on not having role models. Even the smartest and most successful executives don't know how to job search or they are woefully out of date. Remember, it's a new era of job search for everybody, so you have equal chance to shine!

For all of these excuses and more, I say, "Cut the Crap, Get a Job!" Ask for help...it's everywhere. Job searching does not come naturally to most people. Those who are overcoming the above excuses are reaching out for help, following the advice by changing their approach, and, as a result, winning jobs.

HOMEWORK ASSIGNMENT

☐ Write down your Job Search Project Name.

☐ Tell at least one friend or family member about your project and tell them what name you have given it. Ask them for their support when you talk about "Fred" and invite them to give you words of encouragement or a kick in the pants when you start getting frustrated (again).

☐ Write down 3-5 positive phrases about the journey you are about to begin or restart. Think about an adventurous trip you are about to take and words you might use: anticipation, excitement, energy, exploration, eagerness, etc.

CHAPTER 2
COMMIT TO THE ODDS GAME

Joe Dayton applied to one job and then waited to hear back from the hiring company before starting another job application. He believed each job was going to work out *"so why get another one spun up?"* Joe convinced himself that *"this was the one"* and that he had a real chance to win...this time. But he didn't win that job. So, four weeks later, he started over again looking at job postings. As a result, it took Joe a *lot* longer to get a job, triggering the negative emotions I discussed in Chapter 1.

Bottom line: If you are not willing to play the "Odds Game," meaning juggling multiple job opportunities at the same time, then don't job search. It's as simple as that. Even the most qualified, organized, and focused job seekers are not applying to multiple opportunities at one time.

WHY PLAY THE ODDS GAME?

Reason #1: Waiting will bring you down.

Waiting and doing nothing is bad for you. It will send you right into Chapter 1, triggering self-doubt and low confidence. You will feel better about your search, your progress, and your opportunities if you have a lot to do. A "lot to do" is coming in the next chapters. If you follow it, you'll wake up every morning with a new task.

Reason #2: Speed up the time between now and your start date.

Do you want a job in six weeks or six months? Do you want interviews within the next two weeks or two months? The only way to accelerate your results is to multiply your opportunities. Even the best salespeople, who *know* how to manage a pipeline of client prospects, are terrible at managing their own job search the way they do a sales territory.

RULES FOR PLAYING THE ODDS GAME

Rule #1: Minimum of 10 "active" job possibilities at once.

You need 10 active opportunities in motion at the same time. If one drops off, add one. You must find 10 job opportunities that are either posted on a website, in a newspaper, or verified as a real job opening. Do not count the make-believe job you wish for if you could design one. An "active" opportunity means you have done something with it. You might only be in research mode prior to applying, but that is activity, so the job is "active." Chapter 5, Build Your Job Tracking Tool, will teach you how to track everything, so don't make up the excuse that this is too much to handle, even if you are currently employed.

Rule #2: Make each job possibility count—or cross it off the list

My father taught me "if you cheat, you are cheating yourself." So don't cheat on how you count the 10 active opportunities. Each of the active job possibilities must meet one of the following requirements:

- You are doing research and preparing your customized application to send them.

- You applied and are within a 15-work-day (Monday through Friday) window to hear something back.

- You had a phone or face-to-face interview and are within a 15-work-day window to hear something back.

- You heard something back from the company, acknowledging receipt of your application, and you are within the 15-work-day window to take the next step.

The good news: Every time you cross one off your list, you get to shop for a new job and add a new opportunity to the group.

SOLUTION

Build your own, personal **Cut the Crap (CTC) Job Tracker**. It will guide you on how to capture all of your opportunities and how to assess if they are still viable. Learn how in Chapter 5.

TRICKS

1 Make it a game. Have fun with the opportunity to "shop" for multiple job prospects versus just hoping and praying you get that one job.

2 Set a higher goal than 10 active possibilities to juggle at once. Just be sure you are organized to juggle them all. I'll teach you how in this book.

MISTAKES

Mistake #1: Not playing the Odds Game. During my 30+ years of helping others build a job search process, my number one challenge is convincing people to juggle more than one job at a time. Even my own son, Chad, a college graduate, learned the hard way! He understood the concept of a pipeline, and he had sales experience. However, once he started job searching pre-graduation, he found one opportunity that was "perfect" and he believed he was going to land. They liked him in the first interview and then flew him to another city for the final interviews. Guess what? He did not get the offer. So he had to start all over again. Six weeks just passed. Fortunately, later, he landed with a great company, but he didn't have a job by the deadline he set for himself.

Mistake #2: Not using a tracking tool. Do you have any idea how many opportunities you may have pending? Test yourself: If you were going to meet with a job search coach tomorrow and they ask you, "How many active job opportunities are you pursuing right now?" what would your answer be? *"About 10"* (*sounds like you are guessing*), *"Over 20"* (*probably exaggerating or many of them are inactive*). Now the real test: Can you show them your list and actions for every active opportunity by company, position, and latest status? If not, you're doomed. The real mistakes are all of the missed follow-up and missed thank you notes you are NOT doing due to your disorganization.

EXCUSES

Excuse #1: *"I can't juggle more than three at a time."* Really? Are you kidding? You need to be able to juggle more than three projects at work, you have the capacity to juggle more than ten other things in your life, and you certainly have or can make the time. I guess your job search is just not that important. Or get organized to be able to juggle 10 with Chapter 5.

Excuse #2: *"I really believe I can get this one job I found. I'm perfect for it!"* In this new era of job search, there is so much competition, both from employees already within that company or from outside competition. Yes, you may be perfect, but there are so many other factors that may prevent you from getting that job. And you will never know why you didn't. Don't waste your energy trying to learn...move on.

HOMEWORK ASSIGNMENT

☐ 1 Build your **Cut the Crap (CTC) Job Tracker** and populate it with every opportunity you have right now. If you are just starting with your job search, start with this tool. Then, every day, first thing in the morning, start with your **CTC Job Tracker**, update it, and assess what you need to do today:

    a. Add more opportunities

    b. Follow up on the current opportunities

    c. Cross off an opportunity that has gone cold

More details can be found in Chapter 5, and the CTC Job Tracker is downloadable at **http://DanaManciagli.com/book-tools**.

CHAPTER 3
SET A GOAL BEFORE APPLYING FOR JOBS

Fire, ready, aim. Pamela Gordon sent her résumé to 9 different job postings and saw no results. Some of the jobs were for administrative assistant, one was as a marketing coordinator, and another was for a project manager. In a few of the applications, she attached a standard cover letter, which restated her experiences from her résumé. To upgrade your cover letter, see Chapter 16.

Job seekers get desperate and anxious, leading to R.A.A., or Random Acts of Application.

 SOLUTION: PRIOR TO APPLYING TO ANY JOB, YOU NEED TO SPEND TIME DEVELOPING YOUR JOB SEARCH GOAL.

You will be amazed at how valuable this step is to:

- ...answer the question you will be asked: "What are you looking for?"
- ...find the right jobs to apply to for greater odds of success.
- ...write an effective application and cover letter.

- ...interview with passion and commitment.
- ...win a job!

WHAT A GOAL IS NOT

When James was asked, "What kind of job are you looking for?" he replied:

> *"A challenging position where I can leverage my skills with analysis and where there is an opportunity for growth."*

Joanne said:

> *"A reputable company that is known for treating their employees well and starting a career."*

Sally replied:

> *"Something in the fashion business."*

John said:

> *"I can do anything."*

Finally, Maria said:

> *"I don't know, but I know I don't want retail."*

None of these are acceptable goals. Let's break it down:

> *"...a challenging position where I can leverage my skills with analysis and where there is an opportunity for growth."*

James's goal is too "squishy," as it doesn't have any specifics. Remember, anyone who asks you what you are looking for may be able to help you! So, the more specific and clear you can be, the better. When I hear responses like *"challenging position,"* I chuckle, since there is no such thing as a non-challenging position. And the job search process is not about you...it's about you fitting into a buyer's need. So, drop any references to your skills in your stated goal, such as "leverage my skills in..."

You may have personal desires like "opportunity for growth, working for a great boss, an environment where I will be learning," but those are criteria that you keep to yourself. I call them "private attributes." Hopefully, you will reference those later, privately, when you have choices between two or more job offers. They are important, especially if you have experiences in the past you want to avoid. However, they are not appropriate for a job goal that you will communicate more broadly.

"A reputable company that is known for treating their employees well and starting a career."

Joanne's goal describes just about every company out there. It's not only squishy and soft, but it doesn't show that she has really thought about what she is qualified for and passionate about.

"...something in the fashion business."

Sally's response is simply stating a very big industry. Industries are not jobs. But it is a start, as it is good to have some interest in an industry or two. However, much more important is to know what type of job, based on the skills you have from your past experiences (including what you are not good at). Focus more on the function or department you see yourself working in.

"...I can do anything."

John's response is the second most common job goal I hear. First, no you can't. Second, it sends a number of bad signals to the interviewer, ranging from "I don't know" to "I am desperate." Most importantly, it shows a lack of interest in anything. Most employers view the flexible new college grad or flexible executive as someone who is simply unfocused and directionless and, thus, a high-risk hire. Hiring managers want to hire people who want their job, not somebody who thinks he can do anything.

"...I don't know, but I know I don't want retail."

The most popular and weakest type of response to "What are you looking for?" is I DON'T KNOW. The listener is not interested in what you don't want to do, either. Keep reading and I'll help you out of this dilemma, as well as how to avoid the other non-goals above.

WHAT IS A GOOD JOB GOAL?

The simplest way to know if you have a good goal is to ask yourself: "If I had a job search agent (like a sports agent or actor's agent), would they be able to show me three positions I should apply to due to my excellent description?"

Your goal should be clear enough to help others help you. Think of it like a roadmap to getting a job. If you were given a map that said that your destination is somewhere in that general direction and is a tall brown building, would you start driving? But if your roadmap said it is five blocks south and the building is on the right with a big oak tree in front, then you would increase your chances of finding the building. Samples of good job goals are in the homework section at the end of this chapter.

 TRICKS

1 Err on the very, very specific side first. You can always edit later. It's much harder to take a "squishy" goal and then get specific.

2 Read your goal to some friends and family and get their input. See if they understand it the first time without any explanation. Ask them how you can make it clearer.

MISTAKES

Mistake #1: Not having any idea what you can and want to do... go figure it out. Exhaust multiple resources available.

Mistake #2: "I can do anything" shows a lack of focus, limited awareness of your capabilities, and is not believable. You may have 30+ years of work experience, but your job goal should be about what you want in the future, not the variety of jobs you have had in the past.

Mistake #3: Hunting for jobs prior to having a goal. If this is you, stop applying and read on.

 EXCUSES

Excuse #1: *"I don't want to have a specific goal since I have such a wide variety of experiences; I can do virtually anything."* If I were texting with you now, I would say OMG. So, you would rather be plain vanilla, competing for a job against another talented individual whose eyes light up when they describe their career goal? If you were a hiring manager, would you want to hire you?

Excuse #2: *"This goal-setting stuff is too much work. I'm wasting time and I just want to start applying."* Go for it. See how far you get. However, I guarantee that if you set your specific goal first and do it well, it will save you time. You will gain time on the internet, gain time writing your cover letters (which you will do, right?), and make yourself more effective in your phone and face-to-face interviews. Most importantly, your network will engage when you have a great goal.

HOMEWORK ASSIGNMENT

☐ **1.** Narrow down your Job Goal. Do research about possible functions, occupations, vocations, etc.

- http://www.bls.gov/ooh/

- http://www.bls.gov/audience/jobseekers.htm

- Go to job search websites such as Indeed.com, Monster.com, etc. Don't apply to anything! Just shop. Don't even worry about the city right now. Find 10 positions or job descriptions that you see yourself not only qualified for, but something that gets you excited. Spend hours reading the entire descriptions, including the skills they are looking for, the tasks you would be doing, and what other requirements they need.

- Print 10 jobs you find. Circle keywords of things in common. Are they all positions that help others (customer service), or that sell something, or that need a lot of analysis? Are they all in big corporations or small start-ups?

- Identify the functions, occupations, or vocations you see yourself being a part of from 8:00 a.m. to 5:00 p.m. (or whatever the job hours are). You will be applying to join a team, even if you are working alone. Where do other people work who are doing what you want to do?

- If you are searching within your own company, find jobs on their career site and, ultimately, be able to narrow down to specific positions in specific divisions.

When internal job seekers came to me for coaching within my own company and say they are not sure what they want to do next, I advise them to go and talk to people about what they do. Ultimately, they should be able to name individuals, such as, "I want a job like Mark Smith has."

☐ **2.** Borrow or buy books on career selection. The web has a variety of resources as well. Joe, who didn't know what he wanted to do next, told me, *"It was a copy of **What Color Is Your Parachute?** by Richard Bolles that saved me. I poured through it and the workbook, completing all the exercises, and it worked."*

☐ **3.** Develop your Job Goal by completing the **Cut the Crap (CTC) Goal Profile**. The download from my website, **http://DanaManciagli.com/book-tools,** will take you through the steps. But how do you even begin thinking about it?

Step 1: Draw a dart board. Think about and write specifically what is in the center. The center or bulls eye represents your ideal next career position(s).

- ◦ Geographic location desired (other cities you are willing to consider, too)
- ◦ Functional area (marketing, accounting, outside sales, operations)
- ◦ Industries you prefer
- ◦ Companies within the industries
- ◦ Size or type of company (small, medium, large, etc.)
- ◦ Titles you are qualified for (senior sales, account management). Note: Do not get hung up on titles

such as VP, Director, and Manager, as they vary so much company to company.

Step 2: List more flexible goals in the second circle on the dart board. What would you do if you couldn't find anything in your bulls eye? Expand to alternatives that you are qualified for and have interest in. This can mean relocation to another city, a job in a different business from the one you expected, other jobs that need your skills, or deciding to change careers entirely. Reminder: these are not 3-5-year career goals, so stay focused on what you can do NOW.

Step 3: List what things are OFF the dart board. In other words, you would NOT accept something in:

- Geographies you will not move to, or maybe relocation is not an option
- Salary minimum you will not go below
- Work-life balance considerations, like commute distances you won't accept
- Functions you really don't want to perform day-to-day

Step 4: Fill in the **Cut the Crap (CTC) Goal Profile**, downloadable at **http://DanaManciagli.com/book-tools**.

☐ **4.** Write out your job goal statement (2-3 statements)

This sounds easy, but it takes some time. Why? Because you now have so many ideas, your goal statement can become very long. When you're stuck, role-play. Pretend you are at a networking event where you are meeting someone for the first time and he may be able to help you.

Question to you: *"So, Mary, what are you looking for?"*

"Thank you for asking. I'm passionate about outside sales for a large manufacturing company here in Chicago. To give you an idea, the kinds of companies I'm interested in talking to are _____, _____, and _____. Do you happen to know anybody in these companies?"

OR

"Thank you for asking, John. I have been doing a lot of research and I am very focused on two types of career opportunities. One is a logistics manager in a distribution center here in Orange County. However, I'm also looking at opportunities in teaching logistics at local educational centers. Can you recommend someone in either of these areas who I can connect with?

In the chapter ahead, I'm going to teach you how to share your goals. **Why do most job seekers keep their goals to themselves as their best-kept secret?** Be proud to be so clearly focused *and* to be able to articulate your goal concisely. But don't start applying just yet! Most job openings aren't advertised. Tell everyone you know that you are looking for a specific type of work.

CHAPTER 4
OUTLINE YOUR JOB SEARCH PLAN

Now that you are motivated and focused on *WHAT* you want to search for, immediately write down *HOW* you will find that job by setting your **Job Search Plan** in motion. You need to commit to a certain amount of time, a certain set of activities, and track your progress. This planning discipline will help you make your job search process "job number one," avoid wasting time, be more effective, and accelerate the speed to crossing the finish line.

A. First, map out your overall job search process, committing to a certain set of activities that you will repeat every day and every week until you land your new job. Be aggressive but realistic based on your other commitments (family, current job, etc.). And don't steal time from other important things such as exercise, time with family and friends, or sleep.

Activity Type	Description	Daily	Weekly
Preparing to Job Search	See the next chapter. This includes organizing your technology, job search tools, communications, documents, and much more.	Initially, 8 hours, then 1 hour per week	1 hour per week
Researching	Internet or library research: companies for my Job Search Tracker, people, industry news, preparation for an interview, etc.	2 hours M-F	16 hours per week
Networking	External meetings: large group, industry events, etc.		3 hours for 1 event per week
	Build then refine personal/professional network list		1 hour per week
	Refine and update your social networking sites	1 hour	1 hour per week
	Contacting network via phone and email	1 hour daily M-F	1 hour per week
Applying or Cold calling	Sending out "Candidate Packets" (see Chapter 15) or introduction letters if a cold call	1 hour daily M-F	5 hours per week
Following Up	Follow-up on external networking meetings, sending thank you letters to all contacts, contacting hiring managers, etc.	1 hour T, Th, or as-needed	2 hours per week
Rehearsing	Build then refine interview questions, scripts for phone calls, email drafts, etc.	1 hour	1 hour per week

B. Use your Outlook Calendar, other calendar technology, or a paper calendar to schedule your activities into specific times of the day. Tips:

- o **Activity description**: Don't just say "job search." Pick a particular activity out of the description column above or make up your own list.

- o Identify **where** you will do this work: library, home, office, friend's house. Find a quiet place with internet access so you can concentrate on the information and capture what you are learning.

o **What**: Put follow-up activities highest in priority on your calendar and first thing in the morning. If you have business cards from an event, follow up on them the next morning. If you made some calls yesterday, follow up on them today. Why? These are warmer than spending time cold calling companies or people you don't know or haven't met.

o **Time management**: If you say you will be researching for one full hour, clock yourself that you are meeting that commitment. It doesn't include travel time to the library, having that latté in the middle, or talking to the person at the table next to you. It's an hour of work. Hard, focused work.

 SOLUTION

The **Cut the Crap (CTC) Job Search Schedule**, a three-week planner that will coach you through the various elements of a great job search process. **http://DanaManciagli.com/book-tools**

TRICKS

1 Have a **routine**. For some of you, it means getting up in the morning, getting dressed for your "job," getting coffee, and sitting down to do Job Number One, your job search. For others, it means going to the library from 5:00 p.m. until 8:00 p.m. Set alarms, use your calendar, and be maniacal about each hour.

2 Set up a **place to work**. This can be a virtual office, too. Grab a box with file folders, this book, and other items you need to work remotely if your house does not have the space you need.

1. **Set priorities**. List out all that you need to do and put an "A" next to the most urgent, "B" for next most important, and "C" for things that can wait. No more than 3 categories.

2. **Turn off distractions**. Cells, TVs, music, children, pets, noises, crowds.

MISTAKES

Mistake #1: Not building a variety of activities, relying on one or two things. Think about this as a portfolio of activities. No one thing works by itself. Even if one technique worked for you in the past, it's a new game out there.

Mistake #2: Not adding newer job search techniques, just staying within your comfort zone.

Mistake #3: Getting distracted. Question: Is this job search really that important to you?

EXCUSES

Excuse #1: *"What I did during my last job search worked just fine."* Wake up! The job search world has changed dramatically over the last five years and will change much more during the next five years. Hiring managers have new tools, and your competition is taking advantage of the new job search techniques.

Excuse #2: *"It's easier for me to do a lot of one or two activities than 8-10 different things."* Who said this was going to be easy? You will never know which one thing found you the next career opportunity, but you WILL know when your job search is taking many more months than anticipated. That may be because you are missing critical steps. And this is like a job in so many ways. We don't get to pick 2-3 things to do during a day. We are asked to be multifaceted. YOU are the product and you need to market yourself in many ways, not just 2-3.

HOMEWORK ASSIGNMENT

☐ Build your **Cut the Crap (CTC) Job Search Schedule,** available at **http://DanaManciagli.com/book-tools,** and populate it with the action items that you feel best fit your job search. By completing this tool, you will:

  a. Learn about job search activities you weren't aware of.

  b. Avoid relying on just one or two job search efforts.

  c. Combine a number of effective activities into one master plan.

    d. NOT do some things you thought were helpful but are just a waste of time.

☐ Populate your calendar technology with appointments to start your job search. 8:00-9:00 a.m. might be "follow-up." 9:00-10:00 a.m. might be "research," etc.

SECTION 2
PREPARING TO WIN A JOB

DO NOT START APPLYING AT THIS STAGE

Warning: It will be tempting to just click "attach résumé" and start responding to positions you find through the job sources online. However, I guarantee that you will fail to follow up, your odds of winning a job will diminish, and you will lose track of opportunities. Complete your preparation first.

Ready, aim, fire. We are in "aim." You are getting focused and organized around your opportunities before just shooting away like the rest of the world.

CHAPTER 5
BUILD YOUR JOB TRACKING TOOL

During his job search, I coached David, an unemployed senior banker, and learned a lot about high-performance athletes. David is a very competitive marathon runner and he showed me how he documented a rigorous training regimen, tracked each workout, wrote down what he ate for every meal, and how he adjusted his goals. Yet David had no plan or preparation for his job search.

When Susan, a pharmaceutical sales representative, showed me her list of where she had applied, it was scribbled on various yellow sticky notes with random bits of information, sometimes with the company name, rarely with the title and name of the contact, and no dates. It was a mess. She couldn't highlight the ones that were still active opportunities versus the ones that just died due to inactivity. There were some she needed to follow up on, but she couldn't remember which ones.

Michael was reorganized out of a job and has been looking for a new position for six months. He has a family, rent, and expenses and has been in "full-time job search mode." He knows he has done everything right since he has applied to over 50 jobs and has a good résumé. But Michael has been through five interviews and has not landed a job offer. So I sat down with Michael and asked him to show me his progress. I was looking forward to seeing someone who was organized around the single most important thing in his life right now: his job search.

Like most job seekers, Michael did not have everything in one place...anywhere. Not in a binder, in a shoe box, or on a computer. He started to tell me about this company and that one and "gee, I thought I was going to get this one." I asked him to show me what he had been submitting to each job application and he handed me his résumé. How about an example of a cover letter? How about a follow-up letter if you have the email address of a hiring manager? Michael admitted, sheepishly, that he did not follow up on any applications and he didn't do cover letters. He thought that the companies he was applying to were obligated to get back to him with some closure or some form of acceptance or rejection letter.

 SOLUTION

Solution #1: Get your Job Search notebook or technology in order. Will you be using a PC? Or are you more comfortable with a binder with pages that you will handwrite in? Or a combination: using a PC, then printing out and inserting pages into a binder so you can find them at any time. You decide.

Tips for choosing the best solution for you:

- DO pick something that you can carry around with you (laptop, USB drive for a borrowed or library PC, binder). That way, you can work on it during any free time you have.

- DON'T scribble on small pieces of paper, like yellow sticky notes, and throw them in a folder.

- DO make it simple for you.

- DON'T start something you won't use.

- DO prepare to be disciplined. If you don't build your organization tools, you are not committed to job searching.

Solution #2: Build your Cut the Crap (CTC) Job Tracker. There is a direct correlation between those who find a job quickly with how organized they are for their job search process. Why? Because there is so much follow-up to do in order to win that job from other applicants. Your mission is to have so many active job opportunities pending that you wake up every morning with a new task. And the only way to do that is to track every step you take; write down every name, email, and phone number you touch during the process and more. All of this will be done in your **Cut the Crap (CTC) Job Tracker** I designed for you and placed here: **http://DanaManciagli.com/book-tools.** You can use the one I provide or build your own. Do something!

If you have already been applying to jobs, it's not too late to populate your new **Job Tracker**. If you are just starting, then get your Tracker ready right now.

What is the Job Tracker going to do for me?

- Assure you have at least 10 active positions in motion at all times.

- Keep track of all contact information, including any introductions that people made for you.

- Build your new networking list of people to connect with later, with thank you notes and professional updates during the years ahead.

- Assign yourself next steps and follow up on the active positions. This requires you to put the date of your next step in your Outlook Calendar or phone calendar as a reminder.

- Force you to cross things off the list if they are dead...and you will have dead ones.

"And what will happen if I don't have one?" I guarantee you will miss opportunities to send follow-up letters to express your interest, you will fail in sending thank you notes, you will get frustrated earlier, and you will think you are trying hard when, in fact, you have only just begun.

TRICKS

1 Be more critical than lenient on the definition of an "active" opportunity. In other words, err on the side of counting an opportunity dead versus believing it's still going to happen. Remember, you can always add one back on or change the status if you hear from the company.

2 Add more than your goal at any time. Never get complacent or believe you will win any of the positions on your **CTC Job Tracker** at any one time.

3 Make your follow-up on the viable opportunities brilliant with each contact! Assure your emails, phone calls, and follow-ups to your network are first class. Don't ever get "casual" or relaxed during the process.

MISTAKES

Mistake #1: Starting a tracker then not using it within weeks, believing "I got this and no longer need the tool," or just plain forgetting about it. I see this over and over again. You don't get to stop using your tracker until you begin the first day of your new job!

Mistake #2: Incomplete tracker, being lazy and trying to only use some of it. Later, you will need some key information that you didn't populate.

Mistake #3: Just not doing it. Period.

 ## EXCUSES

Excuse #1: *"What I did during my last job search worked just fine."* Yellow sticky notes, committing some things to memory, reacting to the hottest email or phone call. That may have worked then, but if you are going to build a bigger pipeline, the human memory and sticky notes will fail you.

Excuse #2: *"I'm not a spreadsheet person."* Well, first, good luck in your future positions whereby you may be asked to be comfortable with a spreadsheet! Seriously, think of the **CTC Job Tracker** like a piece of graph paper with columns and rows that need to be filled in. The beauty is that I designed the graph paper for you and you can use your PC or borrow a PC at the library. I don't care if you just print out multiple copies and handwrite the contents! Just do something.

HOMEWORK ASSIGNMENT

☐ **1.** Build your binder or PC organizing tool (Microsoft Office Word Document file, Microsoft OneNote, Microsoft Excel). The BEST overall Job Search Organizer is Microsoft OneNote. I have built a **Cut the Crap (CTC) Search Organizer** for you, found at **http://DanaManciagli.com/book-tools**. This Search Organizer has all of the tools mentioned throughout this book in one Microsoft OneNote file, including the **CTC Job Tracker** from this chapter.

Think of the Search Organizer as your online binder or box of "stuff." The **CTC Search Organizer**, either using a PC or a binder with paper, will be the one location where all of your job search information, preparation, statuses, and action items will all be found.

If you are using a PC as your primary tool, you will need access to Microsoft Word, Microsoft Outlook Mail (or an alternative mail tool), Microsoft Outlook Calendar (or an alternative calendar tool), and Microsoft OneNote.

If you have a smartphone, be sure your calendar items on your PC download to your smartphone so you don't miss an action. All Microsoft applications, including OneNote, are available on your smartphone, as well as storable in the Cloud via Microsoft SkyDrive.

☐ **2.** Build your **Cut the Crap (CTC) Job Tracker,** available at **http://DanaManciagli.com/book-tools.**

  ○ Populate your name, the date, and save it to a folder on your PC.

CTC* Job Tracker

<Your Name>

Updated As Of <Today's Date>

Job Opportunity #	Status	Company Information		Job Specifications				
		Company	Company Website - General	Job Title, Department	Job Posting #	Job Posting Web Link	Name of Job Contact (if available)	Da... Ap...
Minimum 10 active (green) at one time	Green - Active Yellow - Stuck Red - Dead	Name, Address, Main Phone	To research more about the company	From the specific posting	Important reference number for all correspondence	Link to the place you found the position description. Search engine, company site, etc.	Could be Human Resources, the hiring manager	Date and ti...
1								
2								

*Cut the Crap, Get a Job!

		of Job	My Follw Up		Other Informationn
			Date of Application and How	Next Steps	Other Informationn
		dlable)	Date and if via web, mail	[1] Your follow-up, which you will also put in your Outlook Calendar or Phone Calendar [2] when you heard from them	Who referred you, what have you learned about the job, who do you know who might know someone there

○ Populate any job search activity that is active right now. Feel free to put in past or dead opportunities so you have everything in one place.

○ For every "Next Step," put the same information in your Outlook Calendar or any other way that you manage your daily appointments. Bulletin board, refrigerator magnet...whatever works so you wake up every day and do what you assign yourself.

○ Be honest about the STATUS of each row or job opportunity.

♦ **GREEN**: If the position is still active within the 15-working-day (3 week) window and you have not heard anything yet.

♦ **YELLOW**: If 15 working days have passed but you have not received any call or mail or you don't know who to contact for follow-up, this opportunity is heading to be red unless something changes. Remember: companies are not required to confirm that they received your application, nor are they required to advise if you are not a candidate and will not disclose why. Don't waste any time finding out.

♦ **RED**: You received a mail or call that you did not get the job, you have not heard anything for 30 working days, or you have no contact to verify anything. This opportunity is dead. Move on to others.

○ Assure you have 10 active (yellow or green) job opportunities pending at the same time. Once you cross one off, or make it red, you need to add at least one more.

o Fill out your **CTC Job Tracker** with all of the jobs you selected from the sources.

♦ Complete as many columns as possible with one job opportunity, then move on to another one.

♦ If you don't have certain information, like an address, do the research on the internet.

♦ Be sure to adjust the date on your Job Tracker.

♦ SAVE, SAVE, SAVE. Although your computer may be set to auto-save at intervals, push the SAVE button (or CTRL + S) after every entry as often as possible.

CHAPTER 6
SOURCES FOR JOBS, ONLINE AND OFFLINE

"There aren't any jobs out there. I've looked." This is one of the top excuses (okay, "crap") for not putting more energy into your job search. True, there are not as many as in the last decade (relative to the number of unemployed). However, during this very minute that you are complaining about the lack of jobs, two things are happening:

1 There is a hiring manager equally frustrated that he or she is not meeting a candidate with your skills.

2 Another candidate just won the job that could have been yours.

In fact, there are so many job sources on the web, it is daunting. So you need to erase this excuse from your vocabulary from this point forward.

Now, assuming that this excuse is gone and you have your job search goal set, you can get ready to spend HOURS on the web. If you don't have hours (another excuse), you need to make them. Job searching can be a full-time job and should be a high priority if you are serious about competing for a job among thousands of other job seekers. Much of the research and applications can be done in non-business hours and on weekends, too.

Adam Taylor was convinced that executive recruiters and staffing agencies were his best sources of jobs. So he spent the last 6 weeks sending his résumé to hundreds of firms, requesting that they contact him when they have a job that fits his background. He was frustrated and confused as to why he only received 3 automatic replies that they received his résumé and only one phone call with an interview opportunity. Adam had no plan to actively search since *"I've never had to search for a job before... they always came to me. I have a great background and my skills should be in demand."*

SOLUTION: JOB SOURCE LIST—FIND YOUR BEST SOURCES

There are more sources online than time in a day. So, based on your job search goal, you need to select the right sources. Get organized first...then go to the sources next. Have a plan to spend a certain amount of time on each source. Similar to investments, you want a diverse portfolio.

Here is a simplified way to sort through all of the sources out there. The following is a list as of this book's publication date, but please see the up-to-date version at **http://DanaManciagli. com/Resources**.

	Category	Examples
A.	General Job Search Engines	http://www.monster.com/ http://www.indeed.com/ http://www.simplyhired.com/ http://www.careerbuilder.com/ http://www.linkup.com/ https://www.usajobs.gov/ http://www.careeronestop.org/
B.	Local Job Engines	www.craigslist.org http://geebo.com/ http://www.jobdig.com/ http://www.jobing.com/ http://www.snagajob.com/ Local Newspaper Classifieds Online
C.	Networking and Job Search Sites—Social Media	http://LinkedIn.com http://Facebook.com http://GlassDoor.com http://Twitter.com http://Viadeo.com (Europe, Latin America) http://BranchOut.com
D.	Company Websites	Your target companies have "career" or "job" sites. Many have search agents too, so you receive new jobs as they are listed.
E.	Local Publications—Online or Print	http://www.bizjournals.com/

F.	Job Search Agents	All the major job sites in section A. above and many others have search agents, and some websites specialize in sending announcements. Use job search agents to sign up and receive job listings by email. All the major job sites have search agents, and some websites specialize in sending announcements.
G.	Your Network	Your professional and personal connections from your past and present including: Ex-coworkers Ex-bosses School classmates Relatives
H.	Industry- and-Job- Specific Websites	http://jobsearch.about.com/od/jobsbycareerfieldaz/a/topsbytype.htm Example: http://www.dice.com/ for Technology Search on industry association websites, too.
J.	Alumni Websites	Your school's "Career Services" section on their website. Colleges, Universities, Community Colleges, Vocational and Trade Schools.

K.	Recent College Graduate Job Sites	http://www.collegegrad.com/
		http://www.collegerecruiter.com/
		http://www.aftercollege.com/
		http://www.experience.com/entry-level-jobs/
		http://college.monster.com/
		Or use "entry level jobs" in your keyword search on the general engines in section A. above.
L.	Part-Time Job Search Engines	http://part-time.careerbuilder.com/
		http://www.coolworks.com/
		Or use "part-time" in your keyword search on the general engines in section A. above
M.	Work At Home Job Search Engines	Most websites in section A.
		Search using "telecommute" or "telecommuting" as a keyword to find legitimate work at home job listings.

TRICKS

1 Don't just apply when you see something. Copy the opportunity into your **CTC Job Tracker** and keep hunting for more opportunities. Searching for opportunities and applying are two different activities, and job seekers make mistakes when they try to multitask.

2 When you go to each source, you need to refer to your goal and identify the best jobs for you. By "best," you need to consider three things:

A. Are you qualified? Do you have most of the skills that the job description asks for? Remember, nobody has all of the skills, so don't worry if you have skill gaps. Your next job will be a great opportunity to learn something new and we will address those gaps head-on in Chapter 15.

B. What do you desire? What day-to-day functions do you want to do going forward? How do you want to spend 8 hours a day? What kind of work do you want to avoid?

C. Does it meet your personal criteria? Geographically, can you get to and from work, or can you afford to move on your own, if needed? Rule: don't apply for something that you would need to decline if you get an offer.

3 Learn. Take the time to go to each search engine's "How To" section and learn how to do great advanced job searches. It will save you time and help you find the right jobs for you. Many job-related websites offer "personal job agents" that can help automate your job search. Tell these agents (not real people) what type of job you're looking for and then the agent will send you an email whenever something opens up in your field. The quality of these so-called agents varies widely, with some sites offering little more than per-category RSS feeds (Really Simple Syndication, an XML-based standard and format used to distribute recent news and other frequently updated content), while others charge a bit of money and may even claim to have an actual human doing the work for you.

MISTAKES

Mistake #1: Having a "squishy" goal in the first place, so your search results come back with way too many items, most of which are at the wrong level, requiring the wrong skills, located in the wrong geography, and more.

Mistake #2: *R.A.A* or Random Acts of Application: You just start sending off your résumé because you see the job posting right in front of you. You feel the urgency and can't wait to get your fabulous credentials in their hands because you're so PERFECT for this job! Will you have the discipline to just put it into your **CTC Job Tracker** and prepare to apply by doing some research and writing a cover letter?

 EXCUSES

Excuse #1: *"There aren't any jobs in my field."* Most people assume this before they look. Then, when they are asked to spend HOURS going to the right locations based on their well-written goal, they are shocked. Maybe you are defining your field too narrowly or uniquely, as well. Go back to Chapter 3.

Excuse #2: *"This seems like too much work...all I need to do is apply and something will come along."* My response: You're just not that committed to finding work. It takes hard work, some up-front preparation, and a time commitment. You will see that, once you get on a roll, amazing things will happen.

HOMEWORK ASSIGNMENT

☐ **#1:** Schedule time every day (in your online or offline calendar) to go to the sources that are right for you, based on your goal.

☐ **#2:** Learn how to do Advanced Searches on each source.

☐ **#3:** Sign up for job alerts so you receive an email when a new job is posted.

☐ **#4:** Log the job opportunities you find on your **Cut the Crap (CTC) Job Tracker** and copy the website link to the opportunity into your Job Tracker too. Some job seekers like to print each one, which will also have the link on the bottom of the page.

WARNING: Do NOT apply yet! You've come this far and you won't win a job by sending in a résumé. There is no goodness in just being another job seeker sending out tons of résumés.

CHAPTER 7
SOCIAL MEDIA'S ROLE IN JOB SEARCH

True story: As a job search and career expert, I was skeptical about all of these social media tools as recently as four years ago. I separated professional networking from social networking and felt that the social sites were a waste of time. All of that was flawed. So, as a complete convert and now raving fan of social media for job search and career growth, here is a summary.

Job seekers can no longer ignore their online presence. Additionally, there are brand new ways to use Social Media to enhance and accelerate your job search. "Social recruiting" is evolving and improving rapidly, so jump in NOW, because the only way to learn about it is to do it. Manage your expectations, as well. Social media is simply another element of your job search "mix." Social media connections are not a quick fix, but neither are job boards.

Benefits of Social Media to Job Seekers:

- Be found. Social networking is simply preferred by recruiters and employers as a tool to acquire talent.

- Identify and contact hiring managers.

- Market and sell yourself and put yourself in front of many people.

- Collect great research in preparation for an application or interview.

- Social media enables you to develop a stronger network that can help you with your career as well as your *next* job search.

Benefits of Social Media to Hiring Managers and Recruiters: How many hiring managers browse social media profiles, and what type of information are they hunting?

A nationwide survey, which was conducted by Harris Interactive for **CareerBuilder.com** from February 9 to March 2, 2012 included more than 2,000 hiring managers and human resource professionals across industries and company sizes. **37%** use social networking sites to research job candidates.

What are hiring managers looking for on social media? Hiring managers are using social media to evaluate candidates' character and personality outside the confines of the traditional interview process. When asked why they use social networks to conduct background research, hiring managers stated the following:

- 65%—To see if the candidate presents himself/herself

- 51%—To see if the candidate is a good fit for the company culture

- 45%—To learn more about the candidate's qualifications

- 35%—To see if the candidate is well-rounded

- 12%—To look for reasons not to hire the candidate

Is social media helping or hurting job candidates? A third (34%) of hiring managers who currently research candidates via social media said they have found information that has caused them *not* to hire a candidate. That content ranges from evidence of inappropriate behavior to information that contradicted their listed qualifications:

- 49%—Candidate posted provocative/inappropriate photos/ info
- 45%—There was info about candidate drinking or using drugs
- 35%—Candidate had poor communication skills
- 33%—Candidate bad-mouthed previous employer
- 28%—Candidate made discriminatory comments related to race, gender, religion, etc.
- 22%—Candidate lied about qualifications

Employers are also looking for information that could potentially give a job seeker an advantage. 3 in 10 hiring managers (29%) said they have found something that caused them to hire a candidate, citing content that showed them the following:

- 58%—Good feel for candidate's personality
- 55%—Conveyed a professional image
- 54%—Background information supported professional qualifications
- 51%—Well-rounded, showed a wide range of interests
- 49%—Great communication skills
- 44%—Candidate was creative
- 34%—Other people posted great references about the candidate

Where are employers going to research job candidates?

- 65% are going to Facebook
- 63% are going to LinkedIn
- 16% to Twitter
- 17% to "other"

However, research by **JobVite.com** uncovers that the increase in social media use for recruiting is a direct result of the number of quality candidates seen from social channels. The Jobvite Social Recruiting Survey 2012 was conducted online between May and June 2012. Over 1,000 people across the globe completed the survey in response to an email invitation sent to a registered list of human resources and recruiting professionals.

- 92% of respondents use or plan to use social media for recruiting, an increase of almost ten percent from the 83% using social recruiting in 2010.

- 73% have successfully hired a candidate through social networks, making social recruiting a highly effective source of quality new hires.

- A large majority of recruiters (71%) consider themselves savvy in social recruiting, having a sizeable understanding of what to look for in social profiles.

- 49% of recruiters who implemented social recruiting saw an increase in the quantity of candidates, and 43% noted a surge in the quality of candidates.

- 89% have made a hire through LinkedIn, 26% through Facebook, and 15% through Twitter.

- 86% of recruiters are likely to look at social profiles, and poor spelling and profanity make a bad impression to a majority of recruiters.

The following are the top three most important tools within social media that you need to have completed to compete in today's new era of job search:

Tool	Why is it important?
LinkedIn	Visibility, company job postings, research. If you are not here, you don't exist for many recruiters and hiring companies.
Twitter	Research, job leads, learning from others.
Facebook	Visibility. Recruiters use the friend-finding search feature.

SOLUTION

A. **LinkedIn**—LinkedIn offers the broadest array of resources to further your career. Whether you are looking for your first job, are considering changing careers, or want to move into a more senior position, LinkedIn can help you achieve it. How?

- Finding companies that hire people like you: Search using your own skills as the keywords and specify your geography.

- Finding work at a specific company: You can become instantly updated when a job opening comes up at one of your target companies. Search within your own network, as well as browsing your contact's network.

- Develop human resources, recruiting, and hiring manager contacts.

- Advanced search features will save you time and deliver the best information to you.

B. **Twitter**—Twitter gives you free information about people, organizations, and job listings. You can be an observant follower and still reap many benefits.

- ○ Start to Follow People and Organizations: Following someone on Twitter simply means receiving their posts, which are called "tweets." Every time the person posts a new message, it appears on your homepage in real time. To start the process, use the search function to find people or organizations you want to follow. Once you find them, click on the "Follow" button and you will begin instantly receiving their updates. The best part about Twitter is that you don't need to get the person's permission. Anyone on Twitter can follow any person or organization. As an example, follow me by typing my name in the search bar and clicking "Follow."

  - ◆ Follow People and Organizations: Begin by following organizations you are interested in pursuing. Next, follow employees in your target companies. The information you receive will be valuable in helping you research the culture and mission of an organization.

  - ◆ Job Listings: An easy way to search for openings is to use the hash tag sign, or what some people refer to as the pound sign, which is the # symbol. The hash tag is Twitter's filing system. For example, if you search #Seattle and #jobs, you will find tweets for openings in Seattle.

- C. **Facebook**—One of the reasons Facebook is important as a job search tool is because every business and brand that knows the power of the web is already there. Recruiters are also scouring Facebook for candidates.

  - ○ Search: When you search for a particular term on Facebook, you can narrow it down to people, pages, groups, links, etc., which gives you wide range of options as to who to network with and reach out to. For instance, if you are looking for jobs related to **"architecture,"** you can simply search for that term and connect with people in that particular field. You can search for people who are architects, join groups and pages, or simply find links that have the term "architecture" in them. This allows you to connect with like-minded people and build a relationship with them, which can help you find a job later.

○ Facebook Pages and Groups: These features allow you to join a group of people with similar interests, provide an opportunity for you to learn more about a company, and connect with recruiters via Facebook. **The first rule of job hunting is to let others know that you are available.**

○ Facebook Applications: There are some really good applications for job hunters on Facebook that allow you to get more out of Facebook and other job search sites. Log in to Facebook, click on "Profile," type the application name in the search box, then follow the instructions to install. Or, visit the Facebook Application Directory and search using "job search," "career," or "jobs" as keywords. You will find BeKnown, BranchOut, CareerBuilder Facebook App, CareerFriend Facebook App, Hire My Friend, and more.

○ Facebook Pages: Many organizations use Facebook Pages to promote their brands to potential candidates. Not only do they post open jobs there, but these pages are often maintained by various members of their recruiting organization.

TRICKS

1 LinkedIn Tricks

- Apply the principles of Search Engine Optimization (SEO) or keywords.

- Use first-person and your credentials will be more exciting than a résumé.

- Focus on the last 10-15 years.

- Assure "Contact Settings" are working to your advantage.

- Adjust your "Settings/Privacy Controls" so not everybody has to see every time you build a new relationship or connect with a recruiter.

- Set a "LinkedIn time" an hour a week or more. Make connections, research.

- Follow target companies and connect with employees. Click the "Follow" button and, on a weekly basis, monitor their updates. Many companies also have a separate tab that says "Careers" or "Employee Insights," both of which are very helpful in terms of finding recruitment contacts and hearing more information about hiring at that company. Many even post the actual job listings.

- Begin your involvement with a LinkedIn Group by commenting constructively on a discussion topic. Or start a discussion if you need help.

- Pay attention to LinkedIn Group members. Don't be shy to click on the profiles of people who contribute. They might turn out to be new connections for you, for info interviews or maybe more.

2 Twitter Tricks

- Tweetdeck.com easily organizes your hash tags and searches into one console that you personalize. This is the website I open up every morning.

- Twellow.com searches people's bios and URLs on their bios. For example, if you do a search on <your target company>, a company you would love to work for, then you can see how many of their employees are on Twitter.

3 Facebook Tricks

- If you wouldn't say something in front of a crowd of 300 million in the real world, you should not to do it online either.

- Narrow down as much as possible based on your field of expertise. If you are an architect, you can use the search feature to find pages and groups that are created for architects.

- If unemployed, frequently post status updates relating to your job search to keep it top of mind that you are still looking for a job. Say things like, "I had a great interview this morning... keep your fingers crossed!" or, "I have a networking meeting later today with a company I'm really interested in!"

MISTAKES

Mistake #1: Compromising your current job security where you are employed. To go undetected, you need to do 5 things:

1. Learn about how to stay off the feed (Settings, Privacy Controls).
2. Don't openly advertise your job search.
3. Be strategically visible (learn all about privacy settings).
4. Be conveniently flexible. In addition to being found and seen by the right career stakeholders, you will want to make it easy for them to reach out to you. Learn how to modify your contact settings to make it easier for people to find you and to see what types of contact you would welcome.
5. Never job search at work. Don't tell anyone, don't work on your job search at work (even lunch), and don't use your work email in social media.

Mistake #2: Typos, grammar errors, misspellings. Yes, your social media communications are another writing sample for employers.

Mistake #3: By each Tool:

Mistakes by Tool	
LinkedIn	Not having a purpose or not understanding why you are on LinkedIn. Have a reason and build a plan to reach your goals.
	Failure to participate. If you do not participate consistently, you will not find success.
	Presenting an incomplete picture.
	Failure to build credibility.
	Bad photo choice.
	Not securing recommendations.

Twitter	The word "expert" or "guru" in your title is bragging and meaningless for job seekers.
	Not following back.
	Recycling rather than repurposing content. It's fine to repeatedly reference the same blog post over time in your Tweets, but avoid continually rehashing the exact same text.
	Not retweeting others' content—tweeting your own company's content is a great idea, but make sure you also retweet content from other people and other companies that is relevant to your audience.
Facebook	Many people fail to understand the concept of leaving footprints on the web.
	Too many people get overly comfortable on social platforms and end up losing jobs and opportunities. Some common examples are saying things that shouldn't be said in public and uploading images that are too personal or provocative.
	Clean up your presence:
	Bing and Google your name to see what comes up.
	Maintain a professional, but fun, Facebook profile.
	Major Mistakes include:
	Inappropriate pictures
	Complaining about your current job or current boss or prior jobs and bosses
	Posting conflicting information on your résumé
	Statuses you wouldn't want your boss to see
	Not understanding your security settings
	Losing by association—watch what your friends post

EXCUSES

Excuse #1: *"What a waste of time...I've been on these and have gotten no results."* The key to maximizing your success on LinkedIn when searching for a job is to not think of it as a job search board but as a networking site.

Excuse #2: *"I don't want to read all of the crap people post."* Then don't. Learn how to use the applications that organize your inbox for all of the tools. It's not that hard and is fun to learn.

 HOMEWORK ASSIGNMENT

	Action
LinkedIn	Set a "LinkedIn time" an hour a week or more. Start with LinkedIn's "Jobs" tab at the top and take tutorials on all that LinkedIn has to offer. Then, you'll be better prepared to make connections and research.
	Find at least 3 Groups that tie to your career goal or networking plan. Join groups within your industry; there are also college alumni groups. First, get caught up on recent discussions. Then, participate and ask for help.
Twitter	Open an account and search for topics to follow based on your job goal, companies, and industries.
	Follow target companies and network with contacts who can lead you to your dream job.
Facebook	Clean up your images and posts
	Take a tutorial how to job search using Facebook
	Use the job search applications
	Cast your net wider on Facebook's BranchOut, an application on Facebook that is similar to LinkedIn
All	*Job Searching with Social Media For Dummies* and *The Social Media Job Search Workbook* by Joshua Waldman and his blog at CareerEnllightenment.com

CHAPTER 8
RESEARCH, RESEARCH, RESEARCH

Anne Harper entered Richard's office very eager to share how qualified she was for his job. She was one of five selected to interview out of 52 applicants. She had the skills and qualifications on paper and presented herself well face-to-face in the first three minutes. Richard was positively predisposed. After the social warm-up, the first question he asked her was: *"Please describe the job that we are interviewing for today so I can clarify any areas."*

What Anne did: Stumbled. She could not articulate the primary roles and responsibilities. She made information up on the fly and did not even have a copy of Richard's job description with her.

What Anne could have done: Pulled out the printed job description from her neatly organized information, placed it on the table, and summarized the 3 key points that she had written on the document or in separate notes. This would demonstrate she had studied it and extracted some key insights.

What Richard expected: A high level overview that demonstrated that Anne understood what he wanted. Richard would have been fine with Anne stating that she had some questions but that this was her best understanding at that time (humility is good). Richard would have also been fine with notes in front of Anne. It would have demonstrated that she took time to prepare.

The second question Richard asked Anne was: *"What do you know about my company and my team, division, or organization?"*

What Anne did: Stumbled again. She could not articulate the industry, what Richard's company sold to what type of customer (service or product), how they were different from their competition, or the various divisions that comprised their company. More importantly, she was unable to talk about Richard's division within the company, even though information was widely available on the web.

What Anne could have done: Anne should have gone to Richard's website, read their "About" section, and much more. She could have printed key pages to bring in with her to show she did her research. She could have written out a brief bullet-point list of her description based on her research. She could also end her well-done summary with, "I have a question about your division when you have time."

What Richard expected: A decent summary, showing she researched his business. He was looking for not only an understanding but some display of passion, energy, or excitement about what they do. Richard wants to hire someone who will enjoy the space his company is in. Richard is also inspecting the skill set of being able to synthesize a large amount of data into a summary. Again, Richard would have been fine if Anne brought her preparation notes in with her.

Within the first 10 minutes, it was clear Anne had not done any research on Richard's business, industry, or customers that the role supported. You can guess the result. Anne did not get hired.

SOLUTION: DO NOT APPLY OR INTERVIEW WITHOUT RESEARCH!

In light of the extensive content available on the web, I'm continuously shocked at the lack of research performed by job seekers. There is no excuse for not doing research on two levels:

Level A: Before applying for a position—enough to submit the BEST application

Level B: Before an Interview—enough to win the job.

TRICKS

1 You may be applying to more than one position within one company, so be sure to keep each research organized and isolated to one position only. If you have to copy the same research into another binder tab or online file for another position, then do so in order not to lose valuable research.

2 Take notes, highlight key points, and summarize the research while you are reading and filing it for future use. Write down at least 3 key points for every area of research: 3 things about their industry, 3 more things about their competition, etc. Later, these will be the 3 things you either refer to in your application or bring into your interview.

3 Don't try to commit information to memory. It never works (and always fails).

MISTAKES

Mistake #1: The most obvious mistake is doing no research at all prior to the application OR prior to any touch point for each job opportunity (phone screening, conversation with networker, phone interview, face-to-face interview, etc.).

Mistake #2: Believing you can retain what you learn during your research. You can't. Get in the habit of taking notes and referring to them.

Mistake #3: Researching the wrong information. If you are interviewing with GE, it's not good enough to say, "GE builds solutions in energy, health and home, transportation and finance..." right off of their company overview webpage. Obviously, you are applying to one of the GE divisions, so you need to spend hours, not minutes, doing the right research.

 EXCUSES

Excuse #1: *"I don't have time to do the research."* The hiring company and hiring manager are taking the time to write a job description, time to think about the skills they are looking for, and time to host an interview process. If you want to win the job and show respect for their offer of employment, then make the time. Certainly, you spend an hour in a day doing something less important. Figure it out.

Excuse #2: *"I'm only applying with my résumé, so there is no need to do research until I know if I'm going to the next round."* There are numerous flaws with this excuse. First, what if the company contacts you the day or week after you submit? You won't be ready. Second, you should NOT apply with a résumé only. You want to do a cover letter and make a great cover letter your first page in the résumé file (versus a separate document). An application is a selling opportunity! But you need to research the job, company, people, and industry in order to make a cover letter great. See Chapter 16.

HOMEWORK ASSIGNMENT

For each position you have on your CTC Job Tracker, complete the required research. If you are using the Cut the Crap Job Tracker Tool, you can copy and paste research information and links that you gather and paste them into your Microsoft One-Note Notebook. All of these tools are available to you at **http://DanaManciagli.com/book-tools.**

Level	Purpose	Estimated time to do research	What to look for
A	Pre-application or résumé sub-mittal	1 hour	❏ Industry ❏ Various Divisions—find which one this job is for ❏ Customer types ❏ Company culture and values

Level	Purpose	Estimated time to do research	What to look for
B	Pre-interview, phone, or face-to-face	2-3 hours	❒ Industry ❒ Various Divisions—find which one this job is for ❒ Customer types ❒ Company culture and values ❒ Growth strategies ❒ Top executive recent speeches, announcements, press releases, articles ❒ Competition ❒ Organization structure ❒ People—the interviewer or screener

Here are some resources to get you started:

❒ Monster's Company Profiles - http://company.monster.com/

❒ Hoover's Online - http://hoovers.com/

❒ EDGAR Online - http://edgr.com/

❒ D&B - http://www.dnb.com/

❒ Securities & Exchange Commission - http://www.sec.gov/

CHAPTER 9
INTERVIEW PREPARATION—IN ADVANCE

Sam Anderson was interviewing for the job of his dreams. He researched the company, had a brother-in-law in another division of the company who could be a reference, and was confident in his sales skills. When Jane, the interviewer, asked, *"If I interviewed other people you have worked with, what would they say are your strengths?"* he froze. He began thinking about specific people he worked with and what they might say. Then he thought about a prior manager and what he would say. Pretty soon, he was all over the place with his answer, sharing random strengths that had no connection or story. What happened? Well, the question was just another version of "tell me about your strengths." The interviewer simply worded it differently. And Sam wasn't prepared.

How about this interview request: "Tell me about yourself." Have you rehearsed a short three-sentence version that is compelling to an interviewer?

The state of most candidates' interview **performance** is pathetic. It IS a performance and there is no excuse for poor interview answers for 80% of the questions you will be asked. It is remarkable that the most frequently asked questions are available on the web, yet candidates fumble their way through them. Even more remarkable is that candidates who do prepare do so right before the interview. You can do this *now*, without having any interviews pending!

This chapter focuses on the interview preparation you do WELL BEFORE applying for jobs. Do this work very well ONCE, then you can review, refine, and rehearse it before an interview later.

You need to shatter all that you believe about interviews and restart. There are no secrets.

Success requires good old-fashioned preparation and practice. And the more nervous you are, the more you need to prepare. First, let's bust some myths:

	Myth	Truth
1.	*The interviewer really cares about what I say... the content.*	Sometimes. With certain questions, such as your strengths and weaknesses, yes, they want to learn. But they are also looking for your ability to articulate ideas, start a thought then stop a thought, and simply observing if your speaking style is clear and articulate.
2.	*I don't want to sound scripted.*	You won't. You will still use tone and inflection to say the words. You will be more relaxed since you know the content. You will sound self-aware, confident, and thoughtful.
3.	*I should wait to see what they ask then think about it during the interview so I can tailor my answer to the hiring manager.*	Complicated and unnecessary. Your skills, experiences, strengths, weaknesses, and more are already fixed. You will still be able to tailor messages to the specific interviewer, but that will be accomplished by adding to the answers you prepare during the interview.
4.	*Interviews are all about the interviewer's questions, not the questions I ask them.*	Often the hiring decision is made based on the questions YOU ask and the discussion that follows those questions. So you need to prepare your questions, as well as the answers, well prior to the interview. Not the night before! Read Chapter 17 for more on this important part of the interview.

SOLUTION: CREATE TWO SEPARATE DOCUMENTS WELL IN ADVANCE OF ANY INTERVIEWS

1 Document #1: Your interview answers using the **Cut the Crap (CTC) Interview Prep Guide**: The Most Commonly Asked Interview Questions

2 Document #2: The questions YOU ask during an interview

INTERVIEW QUESTIONS AND YOUR ANSWERS

Following "listening," a huge part of answering interview questions well is to understand why the interviewer is asking this question. Once you put yourself in their shoes and understand their intent, you will be able to provide answers that are truthful yet formulated in such a way that you perform well throughout the hour.

The following is a quick guide to help explain what I mean by the interviewer's "intent:"

	Interviewer Question	What The Interviewer's *Intent* is:	Answering Tips
1.	*Tell me about yourself.*	Are you concise, clear, and stay at the right level versus too much detail?	Education
		Is what you are providing relevant to me and my job description?	Career
		If this is an executive position, are you senior enough?	Current Situation
2.	*What are your strengths? Or what would your coworkers say are your strengths?*	Are you confident but not cocky?	Work-related strengths (not too personal)
		Are these strengths matching what I am looking for or relevant to my position?	Be prepared to give example scenarios of each one, if asked
		If an executive, are your strengths "big" enough to be successful in this "big" job?	Select 3 strengths that are relevant to the position

	Interviewer Question	What The Interviewer's *Intent* is:	Answering Tips
3.	What are your weaknesses? Or what would your co-workers say are your weaknesses?	Are you self-aware and self-critical?	Work-related weaknesses (not too personal)
		Are the weaknesses huge barriers in this particular role I am interviewing for?	Be prepared to give example scenarios of each one, if asked
		Do you have at least 3 or are you too cocky to think they have that many, if not more?	
4.	Why did you leave your company?	Can you be concise and summarize this for every job?	Developing my career and as an individual...
		Are you taking responsibility and accountability for what you learned?	If downsized, stay upbeat and brief
		Are you positive versus negative about a prior company or boss?	If fired, have a solid explanation, staying positive
5.	What do you know about us?	Did you do any research?	Brief business overview, focusing on their division within a bigger entity
		Are you passionate about working for us?	Growth strategies
		Are you current or did you assume you know us from your prior experience?	Market position—leader versus competition
6.	Why do you want this job?	Are you passionate about working for us? (verbal and non-verbal clues)	Link company mission to your career goals
		Do you understand the tasks you will be doing and do I believe you can be successful at those?	Market leader, innovator, making an impact
		If you are an executive, are you talking about the impact you can make, working with a team of other executives?	Focus on the company, not on your skills
7.	Why are you qualified for this job?	Do you understand the job description?	Select 3 important skills THEY are looking for and share your strength in those three.
		Can you show me at least 3 reasons that you have the skills and experiences that meet or exceed what I have asked for?	Same as above.
		Do you have quantitative examples of your qualifications, not just qualitative?	"You are looking for X years of Y type of experience. I have Z years doing advanced..."

Use the **Cut the Crap (CTC) Interview Prep Guide** found at **http://DanaManciagli.com/book-tools**: The Most Commonly Asked Interview Questions

THE QUESTIONS YOU ASK DURING AN INTERVIEW

The questions you ask in an interview can help you OR knock you out of the running.

Joseph had an hour-long interview at 8:00 a.m. with the hiring manager, Susan, for a position he really wanted. He did some research on the company, reread the job description, and brushed up on his top strengths and weaknesses. He was on time and did well during the interview. Until the last 15 minutes. Susan asked, *"Well, Joseph, what questions do you have for me?"*

Joseph displayed "crap" in the form of mistakes that sabotaged his odds of winning this job.

Mistake #1: He didn't have any questions prepared.

Solution #1: Prepare your questions, write them down, and bring the piece of paper in with you to the interview.

Mistake #2: Joseph asked, *"What is the starting salary?"*

Solution #2: Never ever, ever, ever talk salary, even in ranges. Your mission is to get an offer in hand. Once you do, you can ask questions and possibly negotiate. Not before. Not to the human resources (HR) person, a recruiter, or to any interviewer.

Mistake #3: *"Is there a training program or structured on-boarding process?"*

Solution #3: Think about the story or perception the interviewer is creating with your questions. Put yourself in their shoes. In this case, they may be thinking, "Wow, he needs hand-holding and may be too high-maintenance for me. I need someone who knows how to do this." If a training program is mentioned in the job description or on the company website, then it is appropriate to ask for more insights about the structure, length, etc.

Mistake #4: *"What does your division or company do?"*

Solution #4: It is still shocking how many job seekers ask this question. With the web, calling people you know, social media, and many other resources, there is no excuse like, "I didn't have time." By the way, in the U.S., one of my favorite resources (that I have referred hundreds of job seekers to) is your local city's Business Journal, both their online resources and receiving their publication. Look up American City Business Journals at www.bizjournals.com.

The keys to a great question from you *to* the interviewer are:

- How can I show a strength through the question?

- How can I convey something to the interviewer that we haven't already covered but it's important for him/her to know about me?

- How can I avoid inadvertently showing a softness in a skill they need strength in?

- Is my question relevant to the interview? You are there for a purpose. Your questions should focus on helping you understand the job or the team you will be joining. Examples: Don't ask, *"What are Boeing's top challenges as a company?"* when you are interviewing for an accounting job in a certain department under a hiring manager who is looking for a very specific set of skills. You're burning up valuable time, you can read those online or in the papers, and the question is not relevant to the job unless you are interviewing for their CEO or CFO position.

What are the best questions to ask in an interview?

There are many, but I'll share my favorites.

- I'm very self-motivated. How will you measure my success in this position after one full year?

- The first 30 days are very important for me to meet as many team members as possible. How will you recommend I do that?

- What are the top 3 skills or experiences you are looking for that may not be mentioned in the job description?

- Of all of the people who have worked for you, what are the characteristics of those who have stood out as great performers?

- I have to admit I'm a perfectionist in some areas. What are the aspects of this position that absolutely require precision and attention to detail?

- What do you find most creative about what you do...and what aspects would have a creative feeling to them for me? (Replace "creative" with another positive skill of the position.)

- *Of all of the criteria you have outlined for this position, what are the top 3 in stack rank order?*

- *The position we are discussing is something I am very excited about. Can you give me feedback on how I am meeting your qualifications and if I will proceed to the next level of the hiring process?* (This is called "going for the close" or "asking for the order" in sales.)

TRICKS

1 LISTEN!!! When nervous, LISTEN harder. Well over 50% of the poor interview answers are because the candidate didn't listen to the very basic question. This sabotages your entire interview because the hiring manager is going to have concerns that you won't listen to their instructions on the job.

    a. Check yourself to be sure you don't have your own set of messages you want to blurt out. This will cause you to answer in a way that pushes your information versus what the interviewer asked for.

    b. Sometimes the interviewer will repeat the question since you answered a different one. Only let that happen once, as they are giving you a break. LISTEN harder from now on.

    c. If you don't understand the question, ask, "Can you repeat the question and clarify please?"

2 *"The Law of 3s"*—For every question, both during your preparation AND during your interview, state no more than 3 things then **stop**. A full stop, not just a pause for breath. If the interviewer wants more, she will ask. If the silence becomes too awkward, you can ask, "Would you like more information?" Smile at the end of every question. Not a huge, silly smile, but grin as if you just hit the right note, crossed a finish line, or got an A on a quiz.

3 You will have a pen and paper open on the table during a face-to-face interview (Chapter 17). In the far right or left margin, you can have short clues to some key interview questions and answers that you are nervous about remembering.

4 Scribble some words about the question down so you can peek at it and stay on track.

5 Pause after the question is asked and think. Feel free to scribble 3 words down that will be your 3 points. Then begin.

MISTAKES

Mistake #1: Not listening to the question. Most of them are quite easy...if you listen.

Mistake #2: Not having interesting questions to ask the interviewer.

Mistake #3: Talking too much, rambling, taking too much time, random thoughts.

Mistake #4: Not taking notes. An interview is a dialogue as well as a performance. The person on the other end of the table or phone is giving clues, tips, and information along the way that will all be valuable to you for future interviews or on the job. It also shows respect.

Mistake #5: Being unprepared. No thoughts about your basic strengths or weaknesses, no copy of your résumé, not fluent in their job description...the list goes on.

EXCUSES

Excuse #1: *"It's just a phone screen by HR or a recruiter."* You need as much preparation for this as you do a formal interview. If you bomb here, you don't move to the next phase. You will also gain some insights about the position and company AND they will ask you if you have any questions for them.

Excuse #2: *"It's a phone interview, not a face-to-face, so it must not be that important."* First, this thinking is flawed. More and more companies are doing phone screens or interviews. Never underestimate the value of this conversation, the influence of the person (regardless of their title), or the importance of your performance. Second, you get to have notes in front of you! You should be amazingly prepared, as you don't have to memorize anything.

Excuse #3: *"I think the interviewer will frown upon me having notes in front of me."* Get over that. They are still your thoughts, your feedback to the questions, and it's your interview for the job! Choose one: Option A, you don't get the job because you fumbled through the interview questions (nerves, you forgot some key points, etc.), or Option B: You got the job since you showed such interest, preparation, and passion for the position. In my decades of being on interview teams, I have never heard an interviewer complain, "Wow, they were too prepared and even had notes in front of them." Never.

HOMEWORK ASSIGNMENT

☐ Complete the CTC Interview Prep Guide found at **http://DanaManciagli.com/book-tools**

☐ Prepare 6 questions you will use to ask the interviewer(s).

☐ Practice both and review them with friends or your job search buddy (Chapter 1), then refine them.

CHAPTER 10
NETWORK FOR JOBS

Elizabeth worked with Brad over 10 years ago and they have not kept in contact. Until last week. Brad is recently unemployed and contacted Elizabeth via Facebook with the following message:

Hey, Elizabeth, how are ya? I was just let go from my company and would like to pick your brain about job opportunities out there. Let's do coffee. What time works for you?

Regards, Brad

Pamela and Sharon, both job seekers, went to an evening networking event hosted by the local Chamber of Commerce. The event started at 6:00 p.m., but they got there at about 7:00 p.m. Together, they got a drink, found an empty table to stand at, and talked about "life." Sharon met one interesting person in the drink line and Pamela bumped into an ex-peer from a prior company as she was getting her coat to leave. On the way home, they both agreed it was a terrible waste of their time and they would have much more luck applying to jobs online at home.

Charles is 52 years old, new to Chicago, and doesn't know anybody. But he loves the city and is seeking a role as an architect.

He's spending all day either on his computer or calling the largest architecture firms in Chicago, trying to reach a senior person who will talk to him. After six months, he is frustrated and insecure about his ability to get a job. His money is running out.

Ryan, fresh out of MBA School, is blasting his LinkedIn contacts with: "I am looking for a job. It will be great if you can advise me on my job research. Regards, Ryan."

All of the above have one thing in common. They have not learned how to network for career success. They don't appreciate the need for preparation, professionalism, and a process. I have been told I am maniacal in my networking process, but I am also labeled the "queen of networking." So here is the Cut the Crap solution for networking for a job:

SOLUTION

#1: HAVE A NETWORKING PLAN

Your mission: to identify people who can help you learn, help point you to resources, or introduce you to someone else. As a result of your work in Chapter 3, Setting a Goal, you now have a clear bulls eye for your job search. This plan will focus your networking efforts on the right people or events based on your goal.

Steps for building a great Networking Plan:

A. List **People You Know**. Look at your Outlook Contacts, your stacks of business cards, recent email communications, and put them in the following categories:

- ○ Current and Past Peers
- ○ Current and Past Managers or Mentors

- ○ Peers or Friends in Other Organizations
- ○ Contacts from Industry Organizations
- ○ Customers, Partners, and Competitors

B. Now, you want to list **New People to Contact**. These people should help fill in the gaps of your prior list or those with complementary competencies and experiences. If you don't know their specific name, put the title or position type (venture capitalist, industry spokesperson, etc.). Take your Cut the Crap (CTC) Search Profile work from Chapter 3 and be sure to add a blank row for people inside the companies you want to work for. You need to meet people who work in the organization you're interested in. Meeting them does not mean that they will hand you jobs. Hopefully, they will give you some insight and advice *and* possibly offer to meet with you.

C. Finally, and since networking is a two-way connection, list what you can offer in return. How can you show appreciation—make introductions to others, give recommendations or feedback, volunteer help, etc.?

My Job Search Networking Plan

Cut the Crap (CTC) Networking Plan

Job Search Goal (Function, industries, target companies, cities, job titles)	People I Know (Those who could help you learn or grow in some way, point you to resources, introduce you to someone else, or mentor you)	New People to Find (Those with complementary competencies, experiences, can help fill in gaps, etc. Could be a title without a name.)
•	Current and Past Peers • •	1. 2.
• •	Friends and Family • •	3.
•	Current and Past Managers or Mentors • •	4. 5.
•	Peers or Friends in Other Organizations • •	6.
•	Contacts from Industry Organizations • •	
	Customers, Partners, and Competitors • •	

This and other job search tools can be downloaded at **http://Dana-Manciagli.com/book-tools.**

D. How to find and connect with your new network

1. Face-to-Face Networking:

People need to get to know you, trust you, like you, and believe that you do what you say you are going to do. It is not always easy, comfortable, or interesting to meet total strangers. You will make some mistakes and feel awkward or silly at times. Dive in. We all do. With practice, you may even get to enjoy it!

♦ **Industry, charity, service associations, and events.** Seek out industry events that tie to your career goals and participate in the following:

o Special Interest Groups, or SIGs—committees to accomplish the association's objectives on a variety of levels

o Annual or quarterly industry awards

o Live monthly or quarterly events

o Dinner meetings and presentations

o Online Community Forums—virtual communities focused on specific topics where members can post and respond to questions, share insights, and communicate and collaborate with other members beyond face-to-face events.

♦ **Volunteer.** Local organizations have great community leaders involved on their boards, and there is no better way to meet them *and* spend time giving back to your community. If you are unemployed and have time to give back, then you can also meet influential mentors simultaneously.

- ◆ **Create your own mentor group.** Bring people together once a month with the goal of helping one another.

- ◆ **Job search, employment, and job Fairs.** Look in your newspaper or online for the local events hosted in your area.

- ◆ **Business Journals.** You can find multiple opportunities by searching in your city's Business Journal (www.bizjournals.com for the Journal in or near your city), local newspaper, or online.

2 Online Networking—Social Media Networking

This form of networking with total strangers is more difficult, takes longer, and the type of advice you receive will be different. But definitely add it to your networking plan. It's harder for someone to get to know you and there is a lot of "noise" from other job seekers. Use social media strategically and professionally. Just because you are networking online does not give you permission to use slang, text-speak, have typos, poor grammar, or just a plain old poorly written communication.

Some of my preferred methods are:

- o Join Discussions within Groups on **LinkedIn** that are relevant to your Job Search Goals. There are many groups for job seekers, in general, down to industry-specific job seekers, and so much more. You can join groups of the companies you are targeting. LinkedIn Groups are a great place to do research too, but some top contributors and thought leaders will also stand out. You can contribute to discussions or ask a thoughtful question and get help. If some professionals appear eager to help, it is appropriate to ask if you can have a 15 minute phone conversation with them.

○ Assure your **LinkedIn** profile is at 100%. There are many articles and tutorials about how to maximize LinkedIn, overall, and there are many ways to job search even if you are still with a company. If you are unemployed, make it very clear on your profile that you are searching for your next career move AND "here is what I am searching for."

○ **TweetChat** helps put your blinders onto the Twitter-sphere while you monitor and chat about one topic. By using hash tags, you can identify specific topics and TweetChat will connect you with people talking about similar things.

○ Some of your **Facebook** contacts are probably good advisors for your job search. Send them a personal note, giving them as much information as possible so they can help you.

#2: ASK FOR HELP WITH A PURPOSE

Get over the guilt, the shyness, and the embarrassment of asking for help in your job search. Change the way you ask for help as well. Once you have a clear purpose, you will use your well-rehearsed "pitch" when at group networking events, meeting strangers, reaching out to friends and family, and in more formal networking meetings.

Be proud of your job search goal you completed in Chapter 3. On the other hand, your embarrassment and guilt comes across as lacking confidence. Diana secured a meeting with Frank for help on her job search, needing help with introduction to some executives. She came to Frank's office door and didn't knock or let him know she was there. They lost 5 minutes since Frank just kept working, unaware Diana was on time. Then, Diana's very first words were, *"I'm so sorry, Frank, I know you are very busy and don't have time to meet with me."* Diana continued with, *"I won't take much of your time and if you can't help me I understand."*

What is Frank's first impression? "Hmm...she might be afraid of collaborating in a business environment, she is lacking confidence, and we just lost 5 minutes of our 30 minutes for her apologies." Harsh, eh? Well, Frank will never tell Diana any of that, and he'll be cordial. However, he won't become a raving fan of Diana's going forward.

Have a clear job search goal and be excited about it! The meeting continued and Frank asked, "So, Diana, what are you looking for?" (Frank is implying, "How can I help?") Diana responded, *"Well, I'm not sure, which is why I'm here."* Not good. Your network is ideally suited to help you reach a goal, not a career counselor. Yes, there are a few who may enjoy this level of discussion, but during my 30+ years in Fortune 500 companies, I learned that most networking is best when the job seeker has narrowed this down herself. There are many resources, both online and in books, to help you assess what types of jobs are right for you. Do your research before you network!

#3: REHEARSE AND PREPARE YOURSELF FOR GREAT NETWORKING

In front of a mirror or in your mind, practice what you will do and say from the minute you enter through your closing summary of the meeting—from the strong handshake and eye contact, the first words out of your mouth, all the way to the closing handshake and smile. If Diana had done this, her valuable 30 minutes with Frank would have resulted in an entirely different set of "help."

Are you prepared to network? Here is a short checklist:

- ✓ Pad and pen for note-taking...don't EVER go to a meeting without it...and use it!
- ✓ Copies of your résumé, samples of your work.
- ✓ Business cards—yes, even a personal business card with your contact information and social media links.
- ✓ A list of your target companies, target positions, target industries, etc.
- ✓ The right attire. When in doubt, err on the formal side. No perfume, cologne, cigarette smoke, bad breath, or body odor.
- ✓ If via phone, do you have a quiet environment, battery power for your cell, etc.?
- ✓ A watch. If you asked for 30 minutes, it's your duty to watch the clock and end on time.

#4: FOLLOW UP IMMEDIATELY WITH EVERY NETWORK CONTACT

This is where bad form gets ugly. Networking or "connecting" is the process of building up two-way relationships for the long term. When a job seeker either doesn't follow up multiple times or disappears, it's called "using."

Rules for following up on networking contacts:

- At the end of every day or beginning of the next day, thank everyone who helped you. If you had a network meeting, thank that person and thank whoever introduced you to them.

- A thank you email should be done within 24 hours OR send a handwritten note. Include some insight about the meeting (from the notes you took!) and have a next step, such as, "I will keep you posted about my progress," or, "I will ask for more time with you as soon as I have..."

- All people who have helped you want to know how your job search is going. Consider them part of your advisory board or team and keep them updated at least once per month. They will be more inclined to continue helping you.

- When you meet an interesting, relevant, and helpful person during your networking journey, here are some recommendations on how to follow up. NOTE: Use your best judgment so you are not perceived as annoying.

  1) Bing or search their name—you can find additional information to help you with reasons to connect.

  2) Write a formal email within 48 hours, indicating that you enjoyed meeting them, and suggest a 15-minute phone call or meeting, providing your purpose. If they prefer a face-to-face meeting, you would be happy to come to their office or a convenient location. Always show interest in who they are and what they do.

  3) Send a LinkedIn invitation, including a note that you enjoyed meeting at the event where you met.

  4) Follow the person on Twitter. This can provide real time data to improve the content of your communication.

  5) Enter the information into your Outlook Contacts or other contact management system. In the notes section of the contact, write the date and location you met, as well as any notes of what you discussed.

#5: MINGLE AT NETWORKING EVENTS

First, set a goal for how many quality people you want to meet at the event. By quality I mean that you identified and had a conversation with individuals who are connected to the space you want to be in, professionally. Are they working in your industry, your field or function, or in one of your target companies? Quality also means that you had a conversation with them, captured their contact information (business card or you wrote it down on the notepad you are carrying), AND you asked them if you could follow up with them after the event.

Second, get to the event ridiculously early. Traffic happens every day, work or family issues crop up, etc. So aim to be in the parking lot 15 minutes before the start time and be one of the first, if not the first, to check in. Talk to the hosts of the event, too. Association staff often know a lot of people in the community, and they can give you advice about other networking events that are coming up.

Third, separate from any friends you know at the event. Simply be honest. "I don't mean to be rude and would love to talk to you, but I'm here to meet total strangers who can help me win my dream job."

Fourth, walk up to total strangers. They may be there by themselves, too, or standing among a group of people. Either way, smile, say, "Hello, my name is Harry, what is yours?" There are many good ice-breakers, such as, "What brings you to this event?" or, "What company do you work for?"

Here are some networking "starters" to help you avoid, "How about that rain out there, eh?"

a. *"How did you get your current position?"*

    i   What was the key to success?

    ii   How would you change your search process next time? Why do you think you won the position over multiple candidates?

    iii One key piece of advice you have for me is…?

B. *"How are you maintaining your network?"*

    i   Do you keep them all organized? How?

    ii   Are you good at following up and staying in touch with people?

    iii What will you change as a result of this conference/ meeting?

C. *"Why did you attend this <subject> conference or meeting?"*

    i   Do you have a personal goal you can share with me?

    ii   Can I share mine with you?

    iii How can we help each other reach our goals?

D. *"Do you love what you are doing?"*

    i   What do you do?

    ii   What is the best part about it?

    iii How did (or will) you match your passion with your day-to-day job? Any advice for me?

TRICKS

1 Get into a rhythm or pattern every time you meet someone new, either face-to-face, via phone, or online.

- o Capture their information in a contact.

- o Put a date in your calendar (or task for those advanced Microsoft Outlook users!) to follow up with them.

- o Put another date in your calendar to follow up with them again.

- o Send them a thank you note within 48 hours.

- o Send other thank you notes if someone else connected you to this person (or an association event director, letting them know that their event was fruitful for you).

2 Color-code your Outlook contacts by event or type of contact. You may even just have a "green" category labeled "Job Search Network." Then, when you land in a job, you have a high-quality database to send out a thank you note to and announce your good news. Most importantly, you get to offer any help back to them at any time.

 MISTAKES

Mistake #1: Dominating the conversation with your agenda. You are there to listen and learn and make an initial first impression so you can follow up with some key individuals the next day. Naturally, if they ask, "What kind of position are you looking for?" then you have your well-prepared, short version all ready. Say 3 short things then stop talking.

Mistake #2: Don't ask them to email you. You are the product that you are selling and you need to drive the job search process, even when networking. Take accountability and use phrases like, "May I send you an email proposing some times for us to talk again?"

Mistake #3: Not reading body language. Non-verbal cues are critical for you to observe and understand. If three people are at a networking event, looking like they are in a heated debate, they are. Do not walk up and say, *"Hi, I'm Sally."* Additionally, if someone is not engaging with you, then politely say, "It was a pleasure meeting you and enjoy your evening." Or ask them if you can follow up with them at another time after the event.

Mistake #4: Not moving around to various people at a networking event. Although one person may seem to be the ultimate network "catch" and they are being very helpful right there, try to move around the room during the event as much as possible. Find that fine balance between having a good conversation to open up a new relationship versus actually having that job search conversation right there. Maximize the networking event opportunity.

Mistake #5: Not dressed the part. Some networking events are business attire or business casual. However, since you are the job seeker, you need to be sure you are on the formal side. When in doubt, dress formally. OR call the association or event coordinator and ask them what would be appropriate. First impressions do count, so I prefer you look like a great candidate than be underdressed.

Mistake #6: Bugging or annoying your network contact after meeting them. Use your best judgment by putting yourself in their shoes. At an event, don't follow someone around or dominate their time. When contacting someone via email or phone, use the "Law of 3s:" If you contact someone 3 times and they do not respond, then you should stop. Wait a few weeks and try one more alternative approach.

Mistake #7: Giving your special network contact's name out to friends or other job seekers. If you make a connection and that contact is helpful, that is not permission to give their name out to others. Protect your black book. If you want to make an introduction, contact your network and ask for permission. Wait for an answer. If there is no answer, assume "no."

 ## EXCUSES

Excuse #1: *I don't know how to network; I've never done it before.* It's time to learn a life skill that will benefit your career success, regardless if you are looking for a job or not. Start now, do something, and get over the awkwardness or excuse that you don't know how. So many resources are available to help. You just need to want to put your actions where your mouth is!

Excuse #2: *I don't have time.* Then finding a job must not be that important. If you work fulltime, you need to be creative outside of work hours. You can send emails any time of the morning or evening (or write them and schedule them to be sent at a later time via Outlook) and schedule a networking event in place of watching TV at home. Key: If it's not in your calendar to do a networking activity, it won't get done. If your meetings, personal appointments, and birthdays are in your calendar, why isn't networking?

Excuse #3: *I don't have a network.* You ALL have networks. You just have not stopped to articulate your goal and map out who is in your network today and who you need to meet. We overlook those who are closest to us or who know us best. Family, extended family, friends, ex-bosses, ex-peers, organizations, and clubs we belong to. And if you truly don't have a network because you are new to a city, then it is even more critical that you build one now.

Excuse #4: *It's fake and contrived and artificial.* YES, only if you are *using* people. That is not networking. And it is so wildly apparent when someone is "using" versus "networking." Networking, or connecting, is the action of building a two-way relationship for the long term. "Using" is the one-way action of opportunistically seeking help from someone then disappearing.

Excuse #5: *I'm an introvert.* Celebrate! Introverts are better net-workers than extroverts. You listen, make good eye contact, slow down, and engage on a more genuine (perceived) level than extroverts. Your hardest time is making that first move: walking up to a standing group of strangers, cold calling or cold emailing someone you don't know, and asking for their time. But once you get over that hump, you are golden. It's no excuse for doing nothing.

Excuse #6: *It's too late. I'm in job search mode and it's not the right time to start.* It's a perfect time to start. Yes, it would have been better if you have been networking all along, and now you're simply asking your team of strategic supporters for an assist. But you haven't. So start now. Just be sure to follow the golden rules: Follow up with them regularly throughout your job search, thank them every step of the way, ask what you can do for them, and then stay in touch for years.

HOMEWORK ASSIGNMENT

❏ #1: Prepare to network:

- o Build your Networking Plan (CTC Networking Plan), available at **http://DanaManciagli.com/book-tools.**
- o Assure your LinkedIn Profile is at 100%.
- o Have business cards, pad, pens, and a portfolio.
- o Have a clear goal (CTC Goal Profile).
- o Register for networking events.

❏ #2: Set aside specific time just to network:

- o Put the time in your calendar.
- o Use the time to register, cold call, follow up on people you have met, and attend new functions or online discussions.

CHAPTER 11
COLD CALLING COMPANIES

Tony Alvarez sent out 25 very well-done cold call solicitations and received three requests for phone interviews, one face-to-face interview, and a resulting job offer. Hungry job seekers are afraid to "pitch," or cold call, a company hiring manager. There is no downside to soliciting employment, even if there is no specific position posted or if the candidate doesn't know anybody within that company. However, cold calling will only be effective if it is done very well. Like all other job search methods I am teaching, cold calling needs to be one type of activity within your job search day. It can't be the only one, but it can result in a great outcome.

I have not met one job seeker who is comfortable making cold calls, emailing blindly, or corresponding with people they aren't personally connected with. However, recruiters and HR officers are always on the lookout for talent. You could be leaving opportunities on the table if you don't reach out. You won't hear back from everyone, but that one person who does get back to you could change your career path forever.

There are three cold call scenarios that I recommend you pursue.

1. You see a job advertised but don't know anybody at that company. You don't want to just apply; you want to win the job via connections.

2. You see a job advertised and you know someone at that company (not the hiring manager).

3. You know someone who works at a target company (based on your Job Goal), but you don't know if there are any relevant positions available. None are posted on their website at this time.

The hardest scenario and, therefore, least likely to result in success, is when you have a target company but don't know anybody and don't know if there are any positions that you are qualified for. You need to turn these into #3 by networking.

Don't give up or talk yourself out of getting these jobs. Add any of the above scenarios as prospects in your CTC Job Tracker. Example: Write "DOW Corporation in Boston" or "Marketing Manager at ABC Company advertised on Monster.com" as a line item. Don't ignore them simply because they appear to be longshots. Go hunt for them.

 SOLUTION: HOW TO COLD CALL FOR JOBS

1 **Professional email:** If you know anybody at your target company (and I do mean anybody, regardless of their position or level), **DO** contact them via email with a professionally written request. Even if they are a "buddy," give them an email that they can forward in case there is something available now.

Sample letter for requesting a connection to a hiring manager for a posted job:

Dear Joseph,

You and I worked together 4 years ago at Company XYZ. I'm sorry we have not been in touch since then. I do need your help, Joseph. I am applying for position <#, title> at <company>, and I would like to ask for your help in sending my credentials directly to the hiring manager. I am passionate about the position and believe I am a very strong fit to what the hiring manager is looking for. However, I'm concerned there may be many applicants and, therefore, I may not get the opportunity to be considered.

Joseph, I appreciate your help, and attached is my cover letter and résumé. I will also apply via the company website. Please let me know if you are able to either send a separate note to the hiring manager or forward this one. If I don't hear from you, I will contact you in 5 working days to follow up.

Thank you very much,

<full signature block with name, email, phone>

Attachment: Job Description and My Cover Letter and Résumé

Sample letter for requesting a reference or referral for a specific job:

Dear Joseph,

You and I worked together 4 years ago at Company XYZ. I'm sorry we have not been in touch since then. I do need your help, Joseph. I am applying for position <#, title> at <company>, and I would like to put your name in the cover letter as a reference. If you are contacted, please highlight my skills around <skill 1, skill 2, and skill 3>. I am passionate about the position and believe I am a very strong fit to what the hiring manager is looking for.

Joseph, I appreciate your help, and attached is my cover letter and résumé. I will apply via the company website. Please let me know if you are willing to be a reference for me. If I don't hear from you, I will contact you in 5 working days to follow up.

Thank you very much,

<full signature block with name, email, phone>

Attachment: Job Description and My Cover Letter and Résumé

DON'T use someone's name as a reference without contacting them, as it can backfire.

2 **Research and use social media:** Go online and do hours of research into the companies that you are targeting. Try to find a contact name within the job's department or division instead of just sending your cover letter and résumé to human resources. Alternatively, call the company and ask for a contact person in HR or recruiting who is handling your particular job posting. It will be rare they share such information, but try all angles.

DO use the web to find a good contact name and try to get their email. Spend hours on that company's website, reading the "About" section, speeches, announcements, and press releases. Then, naturally, spend hours on the rest of the web, including LinkedIn for connections and more. Once you find a name, you may call the receptionist to confirm that person is still in that role or at that company.

DON'T send a follow-up letter to "Dear Human Resources." Yes, apply, even if you believe your application will land in human resources or recruiting...that is a good thing. However, don't send a separate letter to "Dear Human Resources" as follow-up.

TRICKS

1 Make cold calling a normal part of every job opportunity you find. Example, for job #123 at Smith Corporation, gather the job description, do the company and industry research, and find contacts either in your network or to cold call.

2 Be friendly, courteous, and clear with your cold calling. Don't dance around the fact that you are job searching and that you would like to work for Smith Corporation in the sales department. The more precise and specific you are, down to referring to a job description, the better your chances of them engaging.

3 When it does come down to calling someone via phone, prepare before the call. Write down what you want to say, have your goals, the job description, and any other information handy. It's not "cheating;" it's called being prepared!

MISTAKES

Mistake #1: Calling a total stranger on the phone (interrupting what they were doing) and diving in with your need for their help. Always ask, "Is this a good time for a 10-minute discussion?"

Mistake #2: Calling a stranger, saying, "Susan gave me your name," when, in fact, Susan didn't. You just saw that Susan knows your stranger through LinkedIn.

Mistake #3: Being squishy, vague, or unclear. Are you prepared to ask for help at all? *"I just want to work at the Smith Company. Can you help?"* No.

Mistake #4: Not trying to build relationships and asking for help unless it's delivered to you on a silver platter. You need to try!

EXCUSES

Excuse #1: *I'm too embarrassed to call a complete stranger; I'm an introvert.* You will be meeting total strangers on the job, so why is this any different? Show your skills in connecting, communicating, and advancing your career in a very powerful and elegant way. If struggling, write out what you want to say and rehearse it. Yes, the first attempts will be awkward and embarrassing. So what? With practice, it will get easier. Remember, your competition *is* cold calling!

Excuse #2: *People are too busy. Why would they stop and help me if they don't know me?* The biggest myth about job search is that other people don't want to help. Amazingly, so few job seekers ask for help AND people do want to see you successful…even if you are a total stranger. Some companies even pay their employees a bonus for finding great talent. You need to stop being apologetic about "interrupting them" and make a professional, polite, and clear request. Amazing things will happen.

HOMEWORK ASSIGNMENT

☐ **#1:** Draft your letters, in your style, to your network contacts so they are ready when you need to use them.

☐ **#2:** Review your Cut the Crap (CTC) Goal Profile and your CTC Job Tracker and block one hour to go through your LinkedIn connections, including second-level connections. Your objective is to identify people who may be good to cold call in a professional way as described above.

☐ **#3:** Wait to cold call until you have prepared your entire job application for that specific opportunity. Have your cover letter, résumé, and other tools completed...read on for more in Section 3.

☐ **#4:** Be sure your CTC Job Tracker is ready to log the cold call and network connections you are making for each job opportunity. Don't lose these valuable names, so you can thank them and follow up regularly.

All tools can be downloaded at **http://DanaManciagli.com/ book-tools.**

SECTION 3
APPLY, INTERVIEW, FOLLOW UP

YOU ARE READY TO START APPLYING ONCE YOU READ THIS SECTION

The reason why you are ready to actually act on your desire to apply to jobs is because you have your head screwed on straight, you are clear on your goal, and you are fully prepared to be amazing and beat out the competition.

This section will give you brand new ways of applying, interviewing, and landing a job. You will not only be the BEST, but you will be DIFFERENT. Noticeably different, yet in a good way. You will not only answer, "Why are you the best candidate for my job?" for hiring managers, but you will also show employment skills they are seeking.

SO, DON'T APPLY UNTIL YOU HAVE FINISHED THIS SECTION!

CHAPTER 12
PHONE ETIQUETTE

Phone calls are increasingly used by hiring companies as vehicles to recruit, screen, and interview. As the cost of travel increases, the pressure for companies to be more efficient and effective during their hiring process also increases. What does that mean for you? You need to be prepared to be as amazing on the phone as you are in a face-to-face meeting.

Phone etiquette: Once you are an employee of a company and attending conference calls or web conferences, you will periodically hear babies crying and dogs barking in the background of somebody's home phone. Or a remote attendee forgets to mute and they scream at their children while the entire call is laughing. That's okay once you are hired. We all make phone mistakes.

However, that's not you right now. You are selling yourself as the BEST product for the hiring company to buy, regardless if the individual on the other end is a recruiter, HR person, assistant, or the hiring manager.

SOLUTION

First, put yourself in the shoes of the caller. They are extremely busy, probably calling multiple candidates in the span of a couple of hours, days, or weeks, and they are responsible for concluding that call with an assessment about you. They probably have some specific questions in front of them, are taking notes, and are only thinking about one thing: *Is this the best candidate for the position we are discussing?*

Second, pretend you are in front of them and this needs to be your best moment. There are a number of key characteristics in common between phone interviews and face-to-face interviews:

- You want to understand them clearly and you want to be heard clearly.
- You want to answer their questions concisely.
- You want to be prepared in advance of the call.
- There is a limited timeframe to cover a lot of information.

There are some real advantages of a phone meeting AND some real disadvantages:

ADVANTAGES OF PHONE MEETINGS:

1. You get to cheat! YES, you can and should have multiple sheets of paper in front of you (don't try to navigate on a PC while talking). Minimally, have:

   ❐ your résumé

   ❐ the job description (with any notes or questions you have)

❐ page prints of some key webpages for the company (About, Divisions, People, Values)

❐ top Interview questions and your 3 bullet-point answers per question

❐ top questions you want to ask them

❐ Paper and pen to write down the questions they are asking and to take notes of their comments, insights, and answers. You will need these for the thank you note you will write immediately following!

Spread all of the above out and mark each one clearly so you can find it in the moment.

2. As a result of "cheating," you should be able to have great answers and express your interest in the position.

DISADVANTAGES OF PHONE MEETINGS:

1. You will have a tendency to ramble. No, you *will* ramble. You are nervous, you want to sell them on so many points, and you have no clues on how you are doing. See the first TRICK below.

2. It's harder to understand the question. There are a variety of reasons this can occur: English as a second language for one or both of you, the interviewer talks quickly, OR the question was just unclear. See the second TRICK below.

3. You can't read their non-verbal body language. You don't know if they are smiling or rolling their eyes. They can't see your hand motions or eye contact. See the third TRICK below.

4. Time will run out and you may not have said all you wanted to share. See the fourth TRICK below.

TRICKS

1 **"The Law of 3s:"** Say no more than 3 things and stop talking. Repeat: Say no more than 3 things and SHUT UP. This will not only prevent you from rambling, but it gives time for the interviewer to write and think. Learn how to pause. Take a breath. If the interviewer wants more, he or she will ask. If you are concerned it was too brief (if you just said 3 words), then you can ask, "Would you like me to elaborate on any of the points?"

2 **Ask for Clarification:** If you did not understand the question, then ask them to repeat it. This is not a sign of weakness and it's important that you answer the right question. Just try not to do this on every question. Two ways to ask: *"Can you repeat the question please?"* or *"Can you expand on the question so I am clear on what you are looking for?"*

3 **Stand Up and Smile!** : Even if you can't see them and they can't see you (unless it is a web conference), stand up when on the phone. Your voice will project better and you will sound more confident. If you have a headset, use your hands, too. Nobody is seeing you, but if it helps you to be in a presentation mode, then do it. I do! Did you know that smiles come through the phone? Yes, when you make a statement like, *"Ms. Miller, I believe I am the best candidate for your position because I'm _____, _____ and _____,"* there is a different tonal inflection if you have a smile versus without. They will hear a more up-beat, positive candidate if you are smiling.

4 **Have the Last Word:** Time will run out. Toward the end, most interviewers may ask if you have any questions. Naturally, you will have some excellent questions pre-prepared based on your research. However, that should not be the end. If the interviewer then says, *"Well, Mr. Jones, thank you very much for* *your time and we will be in touch,"* then you want to interject. *"Ms. Miller, thank you very much for your time. I would like to reinforce that I am passionate about this position and believe I have the skills to be successful in this role. Do you believe I will go to the next step in the hiring process?"*

1. You have shared your high interest in this role. Remember, hiring managers want to hire candidates who really want their position.

2. You have "gone for the close," a sales term that means you asked for their business. In this case, you asked if you could continue this hiring process.

5 *Block Prep and Travel Time:* Block 30 minutes before the phone interview and 30 minutes after the phone interview in your calendar. A common excuse I hear for being 5 minutes late for a phone interview is, *"Sorry, I was on another call."* Well, then you should not have accepted one of the times since they were back to back.

6 *Script Your Outbound Calls:* The nice part about the phone is that they can't see you reading from your "script." So write your script. Regardless of whether the person picks up the phone or if you get their voicemail, you will be clear, concise, and action-oriented. Now, write out the email that will follow this phone call so that the minute you hang up from the phone, you can push "send" or make minor changes based on the results of the phone conversation.

7 *Leave Great Voicemails:* It will be rare that you get the person on the phone, so look at voicemail as a great opportunity. Some rules:

- Introduction: Make one. Don't assume they recognize your voice. *"Hello, this is Jane Miller..."*

- Clarity: Pick up your handset, avoid ear buds, and don't be driving in a car or calling from airports or noisy areas.

- Pace: Speak slowly and articulate more than you would in normal conversation.

- Engaging First Sentences: *"Hello, this is Jane Miller. Doug, you and I met at an industry event six months ago and I'm calling to ask for your help. I'd like to apply for the marketing manager position at your company and am requesting your help in navigating my way to the hiring manager."*

- Brevity: This voicemail is not replacing an email you will follow up with. It is an introduction to an email you will send. Do not assume the listener is writing anything down, either. They could be listening while in their car or at the airport.

- Call to Action and Close: Close every voicemail with the next step that YOU'RE going to take. I have received so many calls that end with, *"Dana, please call me back at xxx-xxx-xxxx so we can discuss."* Or, worse: *"Let's discuss."* I call those "plops." You just plopped the follow-through on the middle of the virtual table, and nothing will happen as a result. Here are some recommendations:

  - Doug, I will send you a follow-up email today with this request and my credentials attached. It will be in a format ready for you to forward to the hiring manager.

  - Doug, if you would like to reach me by phone, my number is <slowly> XXX-XXX-XXXX. Again, it's Jane Miller at XXX-XXX-XXXX.

  - Thank you very much, in advance, Doug.

    - ♦ If an Administrative Assistant answers, ask them to put you into their boss's voicemail instead of having them take a message.

8 *Have Professional Phone Behavior:*

- Change your voicemail message to say *"Hello, this is James Smith and I'm sorry I missed your call. Please leave a message and phone number and I will respond as soon as possible."* Check your voicemails often and play them **in their entirety** prior to calling the person back.

- When answering your phone "live," unless you are sure you know the call is *not* a job search-related call, always answer, "Hello, this is James." They will appreciate your professionalism.

9 *Be Ready for Video*: Have interview-appropriate attire on above the waist. See Chapter 17 on interview attire. Even though the phone call arranger says "phone meeting," more and more of them are becoming video phone calls. If they use Skype, that is an indicator that it will be video. However, even if you are sent a link to a conference call, that, too, may end up on video. Better to be over-prepared and ready to be seen.

 MISTAKES

Mistake #1: Being late. Yes, it happens all the time, even for a phone interview. "Sorry, there was traffic, my last call went long," or some other excuse.

Mistake #2: Missing the call entirely because of time-zone confusion. It is your job to clarify the time zone in advance. Figure that out.

Mistake #3: Your phone goes dead, headset dies, PC battery dies on a web conference, etc.

Mistake #4: Dogs barking, babies crying, airport announcements, TV on in the background, etc.

EXCUSES

Excuse #1: *"I don't have a quiet place to have a phone interview."* Find one. Worst case: the inside of your car, parked in a quiet place. You'll need to arrange your preparation documents wherever you are as well. OR ask a friend if you can come over to take the call. If you can't find a place, then finding a job is just not that important to you.

Excuse #2: *"I don't do well on the phone; it's too hard for me."* Learn how. This is the trend, not only for winning a job, but for networking, too. And guess what? Interviewers are observing your phone skills, since your job may require you to host numerous phone calls with customers, partners, peers, and managers from all around the country or the world. So if this is hard, you may not have the skills for the job.

Excuse #3: *"I keep leaving voicemails but I'm not getting any return calls."* In today's era, people take longer to reply to voice messages than other types of communication. When it was introduced in the early 1980s, voicemail was hailed as the number one productivity tool. But in an age of instant information, the burden of having to hit the playback button or dial into a mailbox and enter a pass code and sit through "ums" and "ahhs" can be too much for many managers. The technology is heading toward obsolescence, driven by the younger generations. Fortunately, voice-to-text technology may ultimately land your voicemail into the recipient's email or text inbox. Text messaging has increased, but I do *not* recommend texting anywhere in the job search process today. That may change in future editions of this book!

HOMEWORK ASSIGNMENT

☐ 1. Prepare your phone interview checklist. That way you can repeat your best phone interview skills every time and not scramble at the last minute. Print copies of:

- ○ Your résumé

- ○ The job description

- ○ Page prints of some key webpages for the company (About, Divisions, People, Values, etc.)

- ○ Top interview questions and your 3 bullet point answers per question

- ○ The 3 questions you want to ask them

- ○ Paper and pen to write down the questions they are asking and to take notes of their comments, insights, and answers. You will need these for the thank you note you will write immediately following!

☐ 2. Be ready in your quiet phone environment 30 minutes before the scheduled call time. Check that your cell, portable phone, and headset are charged. Make a call to a friend to check that the audio is loud and clear, ask family members to be quiet, let the dog out, etc. Never schedule an interview from an airport, a coffee house, or driving along in your car. And never eat or chew gum while on the phone. It comes through loud and clear.

☐ 3. If using a different phone, turn your cell OFF during the call.

☐ 4. If using a computer for a phone or web conference **or** to reference information, turn off computer alerts and all other applications, including pop-ups for new email messages. These are called "desktop alerts," and if you don't know how to control them, type "desktop alerts" into the search bar on Microsoft.com and you will see how easy it is to turn them off and back on again.

CHAPTER 13
EMAIL ETIQUETTE

Email is unequivocally the number one technology you must be brilliant at throughout your job search process. It is the main vehicle by which you will network, apply, follow up, send thanks, and negotiate your offer. What does that mean for you? It can only mean one of two things: You are already fluent with formal email communication techniques and this is good news OR you need to learn new skills in order to land the job of your dreams. Most candidates are in category number two, and their job-search-related emails today are hurting their odds of winning a job.

Because younger candidates are accustomed to online and cell-phone messaging, their abbreviated language is natural and they are unaware it is perceived as disrespectful.

 ## SOLUTION

First, put yourself in the shoes of the email recipient. This should be easy because you have received emails that range from excellent to those you can't wait to delete. For job search scenarios, your recipients are extremely busy, paging through hundreds of emails per day, and have multiple priorities aside from hiring this one position. Even worse, they feel huge pressure to hire the best candidate, as the cost of a bad hire is very high. So they have little to no tolerance for poorly written emails.

Second, pretend you are standing in front of them or in front of a hiring committee reading your email. Additionally, visualize that each of them has your email in front of them in printed version. So you should aspire to come across clear, confident, knowledgeable, and capable of filling their position.

Finally, your emails are a reflection of how your emails will be IF you are hired for that job. Therefore, if you have typos, are too casual, or have grammatical errors, their only assumption is that your work-related emails will have the same characteristics. Naturally, this works in your advantage if your emails are perfect. Candidates, they need to be perfect. Every time.

REQUIREMENTS FOR JOB SEARCH RELATED EMAILS (ANY EMAIL, NOT JUST COVER LETTERS!):

Write to a Specific Person. When emailing companies or a recruiter or networker for a job, you should send your email to a specific person rather than the "info" or "HR" address. You'll get a lot more responses this way. If you have a person's name but not their email address, direct the "info@" email to your person in the subject and salutation (Dear Mr. Smith) with the hopes that the company recipient will forward it to him. Job seekers may be able to locate the right person online. Search Bing or LinkedIn. Even an attempt is better than the lousy "Dear Sir" or "Dear Madam."

Make the Subject Line Work for You. The best subject lines are "Applicant for Job ######, Sarah Jones" or "Sarah Jones

Credentials for Job Posting #####" or "Marketing Manager at GE, <Position Code> - Sarah Jones."

Blank subject lines or generic ones like "Job Applicant" can go into spam or be the victim of the dreaded delete button. Real examples of poor ones I have received are "interested in your job" and "Hire Me!"

Salutations must be Formal. The salutation should be Dear Ms./Mr. Johnson. If you don't have a name, then use "Dear Hiring Manager."

Formal Business Letter Structure: If you are a novice at writing business letters, then go to Microsoft.com and type "business letter template." There is a structured format. Your email body should essentially be a cover letter explaining who you are and why you would be good for the position. It is okay to have the cover letter in the body of the email as well as attached.

Complete Email Signature is Very Important: The signature block in your email can be automatically set in your Outlook options under "Mail." Most candidates just sign "Bill" or "Bill Smith." But, job seekers, the outcome you want with your email is for the reader to forward it to other people within their company, right? So put your email address in the signature, since it will be lost once your email is forwarded. Add your phone, your address, and your LinkedIn profile link, if you have one.

Send from a PC: Mobile devices will be used more and more in the job search process over the next 5 years. However, today, do NOT send a job search communication of any type via your mobile phone. It gives the perception that you are conducting your job search from a car, walking down the street, or in between something else more important. Hiring managers don't want to see "Sent from my Windows Phone," "sent from my iPhone," etc. Most importantly, your signature bar is usually missing.

TRICKS

1. **"The Law of 3s:"** Like phone etiquette, try to say no more than 3 things in an email, then close the email with your next step commitment. This will not only prevent you from rambling, but it will be helpful for the recipient to digest your main points.

2. **Send your email to yourself first:** There is no better way to wear the shoes of your recipient than to send the draft to you first. Open it, read it out loud to catch mistakes, and print it to see how it looks as a printed document. I guarantee you will find things to edit.

3. **Count the number of times you use "I" versus "You."** Remember, this job search is not about you. This communication, regardless if it is an application, a network, or a follow-up, is all about *them* and how you believe you can be the best candidate and employee for *them*.

4. **Write in Microsoft Word then copy to email:** Write your business letter in Microsoft Word then copy and paste that letter into your email body. This accomplishes two things: one, you have a saved copy of your letter in your documents folder and, two, it will look nicer.

5. **Proofread, proofread, and proofread again:** Check for proper spelling, grammar, punctuation, capitalization, *and* typing errors. All recruiters and hiring managers continue to be amazed at the amount of typos, missing commas, and run-on sentences. How should you proofread?

   - Read the email to yourself out loud.
   - Send it to a friend or family member.

○ Read it backwards.

○ Correct all red, blue, and green squiggles that Microsoft generates for you.

6. **When following up, attach the old message(s):** So often, when I receive a follow-up to a job inquiry, I get a fresh email from the candidate. "Ms. Manciagli, I sent you my résumé two weeks ago and I am writing to follow up." Always make it easy for the recipient to engage! Send your follow-up as a forward of the prior email. AND reattach any attachments, such as your cover letter and résumé.

7. **Bullet points are king:** Very few people like to pour through long, wordy emails. In the main body of your email, use bullet points to send your key points. The opening and closing sentences should be full sentences, but the core can be bullet points.

8. **See the next chapter,** "Cover Letter Overhaul," for more tricks if your email is a cover letter.

 MISTAKES

Mistake #1: Using spam blockers. Spam blockers are special systems (usually a program or a filter) that prevent spam from entering your email inbox. It typically requires people to fill out a form and ask for your permission before your email will go through. Disable it now! If recruiters, networkers, or employers want to reach you, do not make them work to get to you. Put up with a little spam during your job search, then you can enable a spam blocker once you are employed.

Mistake #2: Happy faces. Never, ever, ever, ever put a happy face or other symbol in a job search email.

Mistake #3: Stop all cute, trite, informal, colloquial, or otherwise "silly" phrases. No more, "Hiya, let's chitchat, awesome, cool, thnx, take care, let's grab coffee, pick your brain," etc. Write as if you were talking to a senior executive sitting across from you in a business suit. Avoid exclamation points as well.

Mistake #4: Email address of "SexyGirl@yahoo.com" or "BillDa-Man@gmail.com." You can create a new, free email account for your job search on Live.com or elsewhere, and I recommend using your first and last name or something professional.

Mistake #5: Fonts are all over the place. From the opening through the signature block, assure the font style and size is all the same. It is okay to bold or underline a few keywords, but clean the document up!

Mistake #6: Assuming that some communications don't need to be so formal since they are "only going to the HR person" or "this is just a follow-up to a recruiter's screener so it doesn't need to be so fancy." Everything you write and will write can be used against you.

Mistake #7: Contractions. "I'm" should be "I am," and "you're" should be "you are." You got the point.

Mistake #8: Acronym Abyss. Follow the main rule of acronyms: For the first use, always write out the words then put the acronym in parenthesis following. If you are communicating that you were an SE for 5 years, then you need to write out "Systems Engineer (SE)" for the reader. Best is to avoid industry-specific or company-specific acronyms.

Mistake #9: Forgetting the attachments. The new Microsoft Office 2013 and Office 365 have a new feature in Outlook, at "attachment reminder" with a prompt that says, *"You may have forgotten to attach a file."* It has saved me numerous times. Just slow down; review your email prior to pushing "send."

EXCUSES

Excuse #1: *"English is my second language."* This simply adds a strict requirement to ask a native speaker to proofread. When I write in Spanish, my second (and rusty) language, I always ask for a Spanish speaker to proofread it for me. Folks, this is not an excuse to have grammatical errors and typos. Remember, your emails are a sample of your business writing once you are an employee.

Excuse #2: *"I am applying for a developer or tester job, and their environment is very casual. I'm concerned this approach is too formal."* OR *"The recipient is a 24-year-old, so I don't have to be so formal—they are used to the casual style."* Your letter is sent to one person, but you never know who else it will be forwarded to. And you want it to be forwarded! In my 30-plus-year career, I have never heard any recruiter, screener, HR manager, or hiring manager say, *"No, he is not qualified because he is too formal."* Never.

 HOMEWORK ASSIGNMENT

☐ 1. In advance of any writing, secure your formal business writing template and save it as a Microsoft Word document. Go to Microsoft.com and search for "business letter template."

☐ 2. Look through your inbox at mails you receive and study what you like about some and what you don't like about others.

☐ 3. Take a course or search online for resources to help you. I brush up on my skills using BusinessWritingThatCounts.com and their great Tip Cards, and there are many other resources available to you.

CHAPTER 14
RÉSUMÉ TIPS AND TRICKS

Never ever, ever, ever, ever apply with just a résumé, unless you have to. A standalone résumé doesn't help the hiring manager and doesn't help you. It is an important backup document and a basic requirement for job applications. You must have an excellent one with accurate information, too. But a résumé alone is not going to get you a job. It used to. Now, with hundreds of applicants per position, screening being outsourced or automated, and email overload, you need to change your game for today's new era.

This chapter will summarize what an excellent résumé needs to have, and the next chapter will share a BRAND NEW WAY of applying to jobs.

First, there are three main scenarios where a résumé is used for job search.

1 **Networking with résumés**: Jonathan received an email from Matthew, a friend. Matthew said, "*I'm attaching the résumé of a wonderfully talented woman who just moved to Seattle and is looking for work. I thought you might have thoughts.*" Jonathan wrote back, "*I'm sorry, Matthew. I would like to help but I cannot with just a résumé. It doesn't tell me what she wants to do,* *what types of companies she wants to work for, what research she has done, etc. A cover letter explaining all of that is needed to engage, thank you."* Jonathan was spot on with this response.

Job seekers, it is your job to *"help me help you."* If you want friends, family, your network, LinkedIn connections, or career counselors to help you, then give them what they need. A résumé simply lists facts of what you have done and what you have accomplished in the past. The reader is not responsible for translating that into your next ideal job definition or where you would be a good fit. Even if you are sending your résumé to Uncle Bob and asking him to forward to an executive in his company, you should give Uncle Bob a cover letter, explaining **what** you are looking for, **when** you are available to start, **why** you are an accomplished worker, and **how** they can contact you.

To be perfectly clear: Do NOT send résumés to people asking *"Where would I fit within <Microsoft> or <GE>?"* Stop. You are abdicating your responsibility for your career to them! Even if you are not actively job searching and just doing research, you need to assess your next career move. If you just don't know, go back to Chapter 3 and set a goal.

Social media sites, such as LinkedIn, are an electronic form of net-working. Therefore, your LinkedIn Background Summary in your profile is the section that behaves like a cover letter. Naturally, for those of you job searching while employed, this is tricky, but there are many online articles about how to job search *secretly* while employed.

2 **Applying to specific jobs with résumés**: Some companies and websites require you to only retype the facts from your résumé. They replicate the fields or draw keywords from your submittal. Other websites state very clearly that you may only attach one document. Option **A**: If they say that one document

must only be a résumé, then you need to do that. Option **B**: If they do not specify, but only allow one FILE, then see the next chapter about a NEW application called the "Cut the Crap (CTC) Candidate Packet." That should be your one file.

3 **Posting on job boards:** In this scenario, the only recourse you have is to post your résumé. For this reason, the résumé needs to be excellent. Let's get right into the definition of "résumé excellence."

SOLUTION: AN EXCELLENT RÉSUMÉ

Excellence can be defined by 3 major principles:

1. **Search-ability:** Key word search is optimized so you are found

2. **Easy to read:** Well-formatted for both online and print

3. **Quantitative:** Numeric proof of your brilliance

1 **Résumé Excellence #1—Search-ability:** You, the applicant, could be the best person for the job, but if your résumé is not found in a search, the probability that you will even considered is quite low. A searchable résumé is key so you can be found in various technology engines such as:

a. Job board résumé databases

b. Employer applicant tracking systems

c. Employer email systems

d. Social media (LinkedIn, Facebook, Twitter, etc.)

e. Web search engines

What are "keywords?" They are the words used for searching and finding appropriate candidates. In today's new job search era, recruiters, screeners, employers, and others are fluent in the symbols and tricks for searching for candidates using keyword searches.

For example, if an employer is filling a Marketing Communications position, the keywords are the words associated with the requirements of the job:

- Skills (communications, writing, advertising, presentation, collaboration, teamwork, project management, etc.)
- Tools (Microsoft Office—Word, Excel, PowerPoint, Publisher)
- Education (MBA, BA, BS, AA, AS, high school, etc.)
- Location (State, city, even if willing to relocate)

Where should your keywords be? Everywhere.

- Filename of your résumé or profile (for those that are emailed)
- Title of your résumé or profile (for those in systems that use entry titles, like LinkedIn and craigslist)
- Body of your résumé or profile
- Body of your LinkedIn profile
- Twitter bio
- Facebook page

How can I make my keywords more powerful?

A. **Customize the keywords on your résumé if you have more than one kind of job goal:** Your keywords can be customized for the position being sought. If you are looking for more than one kind of job (more than one target job title), the résumé used for each job should be directly related to the keywords appropriate for that job.

B. **Add more nouns:** Nouns? But we were all taught to use "power verbs," such as "developed, collaborated, designed, and led." But the "what" that you performed, the **action**, is just as important. In the following examples, the bold nouns are the keywords that relate to the action indicated by the verbs:

- o Led global **cross-functional teams** for plan review and sign-off.
- o Designed and executed online **marketing campaigns** and **events**.
- o Managed **advertising agencies, $1M+ budgets**, and **cost analysis**.
- o Functioned in lead **project management role**.
- o Oversaw **editorial calendar, content distribution**, and **competitive analysis**

There are many good articles about keywords for résumés online, so please spend more time in mastering this critical NEW job search criteria. The simplest way to learn what the best keywords are for your job target is to read job descriptions! Example: *Seeking experienced Accounts Receivables Manager to oversee accounts, manage billing and collections, train accounting and clerical staff, develop status reports for management, and prepare monthly balance sheets. BA degree or AA degree with minimum of 2 years' experience required.* Your résumé should have these keywords.

2 Résumé Excellence #2—Easy to Read:

The content of your résumé is by far the most important factor. But design is important, too, for a couple of reasons:

- Your résumé must be easy to read, and good design makes that possible. Design calls attention to key sections of your résumé, such as work experience and education.

- A well-designed résumé reflects positively on your skills. Sloppy or careless design may give a negative impression, even if you're well-qualified.

There are several techniques you can use to create a highly readable and attractive résumé. The table below lists some of the most important.

Technique	Why It's Important
White space	*Lots of white space makes text easier to read. Text that's too dense may discourage time-pressed readers from reading further.*
Bullets	*Bulleted text allows you to break down complex information into readable chunks and also highlight key points.*
Easy-to-scan headings	*Your reader should be able to quickly locate key areas on your résumé, such as education, without extensive searching.*
Limited number of fonts	*Use no more than two fonts styles—one for headings and the other for body text. More than that is distracting.*
Selective use of bold	*Use bold carefully and consistently. For example, if you bold the name of one company you've worked for, do it in all cases.*
No underlining (except links)	*Reserve underlined text for web links. If you need to emphasize something, use bold.*
Consistent spacing	*Use the same amount of space before and after headings, between bullets, etc. This gives your résumé a uniform look.*

There are thousands of great examples on the web. Add this to your job search schedule as an area to spend time on. For those of you really stuck, invest in a résumé writing service.

Creating a plain-text résumé

Although most companies will be able to handle your résumé in Word or PDF format, you may need to have a plain-text résumé that's been stripped of formatting. To create one, follow these steps:

* Copy your résumé into a plain text editor like Notepad, which should be available as an accessory on your computer. Most of the formatting should be gone.

* Change any remaining bullets to asterisks, and space once after the asterisk.

* For your main section headings, such as Work Experience, change to all caps so the headings stand out.

* Add spacing between sections as necessary for readability.

See this sample plain-text résumé for Beth Smith, an administrative assistance seeking work as a project coordinator.

```
BETH SMITH, CAPM

215 W. State Street, Milwaukee, WI 53201
bethsmith@comcast.net
www.linkedin.com/beth-smith
Cell: 555-263-1678

PROJECT COORDINATOR

Highly motivated, tech-savvy professional with
over 5 years' experience in a fast-paced consult-
ing environment. Extensive experience supporting
senior consultants in high-profile technology proj-
ects. Exceptional analytical ability and talent
for managing information. Certified Associate in
Project Management (CAPM) certification.
```

Proficient in:

* Project Coordination

* Project Setup & Monitoring

* Project Communication

* Microsoft SharePoint

* Microsoft Project

* Microsoft Excel

PROFESSIONAL EXPERIENCE

2005-Present: Senior Administrative Assistant, Grant Technology Consulting. Advanced administrative and project support for senior-level consultants.

Project Coordination/Management

* Led a project to streamline and reorganize SharePoint project management system, resulting in more accessible information and enhanced support for clients.

* Coordinated project plan, scheduling, and budgeting for small but high-profile project during project manager's absence. Praised for initiative and problem-solving abilities.

Advanced Administrative Support

* Prepared best-practice guidelines for archiving project documents. Guidelines simplified document management process and were adopted company-wide.

* Conducted research and trained staff on new techniques for document versioning that significantly reduced retrieval time and lost documents.

2001-2005: Administrative Assistant, Training Solutions, Inc. Advanced administrative support to top marketing executive in fast-paced training start-up company.

Project Coordination/Management

* Coordinated the research and production of client-winning training proposals.

* Streamlined proposal development process, resulting in significant time savings.

Advanced Administrative Support

* Planned and assembled materials for high-profile client meetings.

* Created new client tracking system using Microsoft Excel.

PROFESSIONAL DEVELOPMENT

Certified Associate in Project Management (CAPM), 2009

Microsoft SharePoint Power User Training, 2010

Microsoft SharePoint End User Training, 2009

Advanced Microsoft Project, 2008

Advanced Microsoft Excel, 2008

EDUCATION

Associate Degree, Business Administration & Management,

Northeast Wisconsin Technical College, 2001

PROFESSIONAL ASSOCIATIONS

Project Management Institute

American Management Association, Individual Member

3 **Résumé Excellence #3—Quantitative**

Hiring managers, recruiters, and HR managers are so tired of "world-class marketing person" or "exceeded targets in…" or "best in class performance." You need to prove your results right in your résumé. Job candidates tell me they will wait until the interview to share them or say, "My successes cannot be quantified." Cut the Crap, Get a Job!

Not many job types, such as sales, can claim "exceeded budget by 12% or $3 million dollars" or "ran a team with a quota of $800,000." However, there are a number of other qualitative results that you can display proudly on your résumé.

You could have been 1 selected out of 500 to represent your team at a meeting. You delivered a major project on time and under budget by X%. You won some awards or have been promoted in a certain amount of months, X, well above the company average of Y. Do this: Think about your soft skills (the ability to meet deadlines, work in a team or independently, communicate complex ideas, placate customers). Relate an occasion where those skills made a difference to your company. Many of you have been assigned to a critical project, included in client or executive meetings, recommended for special training, or asked to make a presentation.

Here is a final example to help you out:

Before: Maintained accounts receivables and accounts payables.

After: Managed over 2,500 accounts receivables and accounts payables, working directly with the Chief Financial Officer.

In summary, when you rewrite your résumé to compete in today's era of job search, look for opportunities to quantify, without sharing confidential information, of course. Think of power verbs, (like reduced, saved, made, grew, etc.) *and* combine them with metrics, such as time (number of months, days, or years, dollars, growth percentages, comparison to market averages, comparisons to company or peer averages.)

TRICKS

1 If you are a *Jimmy*, don't put *James* on your résumé or cover letter. When recruiters, screeners, or hiring managers want to call you, they want to address you and get to know you by the name you want to be called. This saves embarrassment later, too. Same goes for your business card, email signature, and everything. The old days of "James" being used when, in fact, you want to be called "Jimmy" are over.

2 You can have a few versions of résumés, based on 1) more than one job goal (e.g. marketing versus sales) or 2) multiple cities you are targeting. However, do not alter your résumé per job. A hiring manager can spot when you are simply plugging in their company name or their job title in your objective at the top.

3 In the date column, put the month and the year so the reader can tell how long you have been with a company. Example: 2011-2012 can be as little as 2 months (December to January) or as long as 24 months.

MISTAKES

Mistake #1: The Acronym Abyss. Follow the main rule of acronyms: For the first use, always write it out, then put the acronym in parenthesis following. If you are communicating that you were an SE for five years, then you need to write out "Systems Engineer (SE)" for the reader. Best is to avoid industry-specific or company-specific acronyms.

Mistake #2: Use of the present tense in all jobs on the résumé.

Mistake #3: Writing the résumé or cover letter in the third person.

Mistake #4: Grammar and spelling mistakes—red and green squiggles throughout.

Mistake #5: Use of tiny, tiny fonts (10 pt. or less) so as to cram as much information into the résumé as possible.

Mistake #6: Photos on résumés.

Mistake #7: Using a résumé that is password protected (without sending the password).

Mistake #8: Using a table format and keeping all of the lines for rows and columns.

Mistake #9: Having no contact information on the résumé or including a phone number that is no longer valid.

Mistake #10: Education written so vaguely that it is unclear if you secured a degree.

Mistake #11: Going back too far in your experience. I recommend 15 years maximum, then a high level summary of the prior work.

Mistake #12: Submitting the wrong format. If the employer or recruiter has stipulated that your résumé or form has to be submitted in a certain format, make sure that you adhere to that. Don't send it as a PDF if they have specifically requested a Microsoft Word document.

Mistake #13: File name of your résumé is "Résumé". Or "432987. pdf." Correct that to "JohnSmith_Position 14254_Boeing" or "JohnSmithRésumé."

 EXCUSES

Excuse #1: *"English is my second language."* This simply adds a strict requirement to ask a native speaker to proofread. Remember, your résumé is a sample of your business writing once you are an employee.

Excuse #2: *"I'm applying for a creative, artistic role, so I want to show my creativity through my résumé and stand out."* Wrong. In fact, even designers, art directors, web developers, and other creative professionals need to have résumés that present information clearly, concisely, and in a manner that is easy to read. The content of a person's résumé is more important than the résumé's artistic look and feel. They are looking for experience and things like technical knowledge of design software applications. Once they find candidates who offer the right technical abilities, they will review your creative skills.

HOMEWORK ASSIGNMENT

☐ **#1:** Rebuild your résumé from a blank piece of paper versus editing your old one.

☐ **#2:** Get some help. Simply type "résumé builder" in a Bing search or other search engines and you will find hundreds of templates, samples, résumé editors, and résumé builders. This can all be done virtually, via a PC, and sometimes a phone, so don't worry where the résumé expert is located.

☐ **#3:** Use the above "Résumé Excellence" checklist to assure you are meeting all three criteria.

CHAPTER 15

APPLYING FOR A POSITION

THE NEW "CUT THE CRAP (CTC) CANDIDATE PACKET AND CTC JOB DESCRIPTION PROFILE (JD PROFILE)"

Whoever invented résumés ought to be exiled. What were they thinking? Let's all document our professional life in reverse-chronological order, spitting out endless facts about every job and adding descriptions that mean nothing to the hiring manager. Additionally, let's share the most irrelevant job responsibilities while painting ourselves as the most versatile employee that ever lived. Finally, let's hope that the hiring manager takes the time to search for my skills that best fit what they are looking for.

 ## SOLUTION

I'm going to teach you a new way to win a job. Start over. From this point forward, build a "Cut the Crap (CTC) Candidate Packet," which you will send instead of a résumé. This is a new approach and very powerful. If you do this, you will not only dramatically increase your odds to be selected to interview, but you will be better prepared to win the job during the interview.

This unique "Candidate Packet" will tell a clear and compelling story about why you are the best candidate for that specific position. You will be doing the hiring manager's job for them. Their job is to compare multiple applicants and assess who will go into interviews, who is best qualified, or who they want their recruiter to call. The fact that you are doing such a thorough job with this new application will differentiate you from the rest of the pack (unless they have read this book, too).

There will be three components to your Candidate Packet that is uniquely written for each job application. In order:

1. Cover Letter

2. NEW Cut the Crap (CTC) JD Profile (Job Description Profile), found at **http://DanaManciagli.com/book-tools.**

3. Résumé

How to Create **"The CTC Candidate Packet"** (*template found at http://DanaManciagli.com/book-tools*)

Step 1: Analyze the Job Description. You need a job description or a deep understanding of the job based on information you have gathered. In order to position yourself as the best candidate, you need to know the skills and background required. Study the job description, break it into major categories, and analyze it carefully. Put yourself in the shoes of the hiring manager who either wrote it or provided the specifications. If you don't have a job description, contact someone who works in the company or find a similar job description on the online job websites.

Step 2: Refine Your **Résumé.** See Chapter 14 for much more on the attributes of a great résumé. You do not need to rewrite or tailor your résumé for each job if you do Steps 1 and 3 extremely well. However, your résumé does have to be great.

Step 3: Write your one-page **Job Description Profile (JD Profile)** for the specific position. The JD Profile is going to compare your background, skills, and experience (from your résumé in Step 2) to the exact job (Step 1) in a very compelling way. It is the single most critical document that will determine your job search success.

It is a one-page document with a simple table of Column A on the left and Column B on the right. Do you remember, as a child, when a random list of items was on the left side of the page and another random list was on the right? You were asked to draw lines between the matching items. That's what we're doing here. Your résumé is not organized to match the hiring manager's job description list. Therefore, you are going to provide the right elements of your background as the "answer" to their "question."

Job Title, #:	Your Name:
Job Specifications from JD	*Your Qualifications, Experience*

You will fill **Column A** of your **JD Profile** with the contents of the job description in an abbreviated format. Bullet-point phrases or short sentences are fine. Group various requirements together, as appropriate. As an example, you can put all of the education specifications in one row. If you don't have the job description, create the information as best you possibly can. A hiring manager won't mind if you take a guess at his job requirements. If you had any type of information-gathering meeting with the recruiter or hiring manager, be sure to ask clarifying questions about the job description or secure the job responsibilities if a job description doesn't exist.

Column B of your **JD Profile** is the most important. In each row and next to each job description skill or requirement, you will put concise and relevant information that shows your qualifications. If they ask for "8-10 years in outside sales," your column B may say "12 years in outside sales: 5 with IBM, 7 with Kodak, exceeding goals 11 out of the 12 years." The key is to answer their requirements and add more information than requested on their job description. You are sourcing the content for column B of your JD Profile from your résumé or from recalling key experiences in your background. Here is your chance to draw out relevant experiences from your résumé and match them with the hiring manager's needs. Always be truthful.

There may be 10-12 rows in your table, and you need an answer for each one. In some cases, you do not have that experience or skill set. Do not lie or fill it with "fluff." Simply say, "Gap area and eager to learn," or, "No experience but will learn on the job." It's good to be humble.

Step 4: Write your **Cover Letter** for the specific position. Now that you have your **JD Profile**, you are ready to write your cover letter to the hiring manager. By this time, you have prepared well enough to address the hiring manager or recruiter in writing. The goal of the cover letter is to concisely explain why you are the best candidate for this position and to provide the proof points. It should be one page and look very formal, including the addressee's address block or email and your full signature block (name, address, email, and phone). See Chapter 16 for the definition of cover letter excellence.

HOW TO PUT THE "THE CANDIDATE PACKET" TOGETHER:

"The Candidate Packet" is a sandwich with three components in the following order: (1) cover letter, (2) JD Profile, and (3) résumé. All three documents should be written in Microsoft Word and put together in one document as one electronic file. Why one file? First, it saves the hiring manager or recruiter time versus opening up three separate documents. Most importantly, many websites only allow you to attach one document to their website. Your single document can be "the Candidate Packet." However, if a website clearly says "attach résumés only," then you need to only send in your résumé.

Once you put the three together, assure it has the following elements:

- Page Breaks: The cover letter needs to be one page and the first page. The JD Profile should start at the top of page two. The résumé should start at the top of page three.

- Footer: Page numbers and your name on every page. I prefer "1 of 3, 2 of 3, and 3 of 3".

- Similar fonts on all three documents. Hint: pick one font for everything job-search related, including your email body and email auto-signature.

 TRICKS

1 Once you do one **Cut the Crap (CTC) Candidate Packet**, the rest will become easier. Therefore, do one NOW so it's not done at midnight the night before an application.

2 On the **CTC JD Profile**, be sure to include skills and experiences that are in your résumé AND include things that are not in your résumé. You may identify experiences you want to add back into your résumé, too.

3 Bring copies of your **Candidate Packet** and, specifically, your **CTC JD Profile** with you into an interview. Share it broadly. If you were unable to send it with your résumé, it is a great packet to email as a follow-up. It is not designed to be your own exercise, but to help sell yourself and package the reason why you are not just a fit, but are the BEST candidate.

MISTAKES

Mistake #1: The CTC JD Profile™ one pager means one page. Not two pages and not 8 pt. font to smash as much information as you can on one page. Learn how to be concise, starting with your written materials. Eliminate unnecessary words or run-on sentences. Remember, your hiring manager is observing and judging every move you make as a sample of what type of employee you will be: written, verbal, everything. This is a writing sample.

Mistake #2: The **CTC Candidate Packet**, when stitched together in Microsoft Word, is missing the candidate's name on every page, page numbers, and the date. Fonts are all over the place. And, of course, the dreaded typos, misspellings, or grammatical errors abound.

Mistake #3: Job seekers tell me, "I don't know how to merge three separate word documents together." Take a word software class, because if you don't know how to do this, you need to learn it! Or get some help, but don't attach three separate documents to an email.

Mistake #4: File names. Make these file names work for you. You've done all of this work making a great "packet," yet the file name is "Document1" or "John's Résumé." My preference: "MattBrown_ JobXXXXX_061760" or "MattBrown_Applicant_JobXXXXX".

EXCUSES

Excuse #1: *"This is just too much work."* If so, then getting a job must not be that important to you. There is a direct correlation between the amount of hours and smart work you put in versus the speed and quality of the job you will get.

Excuse #2: *"All they ask for is a résumé, so that's all I can send."* Take risks, submit the BEST application you can, realizing that others may be submitting something far more powerful than a resume alone.

Excuse #3: *"When I start the JD Profile, I realize I don't have what they are looking for, so I'm not going to fill it out."* Sometimes, doing the JD Profile is great for that purpose. When we read job descriptions for the first time, we read what we want to read. We want to see ourselves doing that job. However, doing the comparison will not only prepare you for the interview, but will also indicate if you shouldn't reply.

HOMEWORK ASSIGNMENT

☐ **#1:** Select any job description that is in your goal bulls eye and put together your first complete **Cut the Crap (CTC) Candidate Packet.** Follow the steps above, in that exact order. Find all tools required for this chapter at **http://DanaManciagli.com/book-tools.**

☐ **#2:** Send your **Candidate Packet** to yourself and at least one other person to give you feedback. Pretend you are the hiring manager, recruiter, screener, or network executive.

  ○ Is it easy to read and well-marked with your name and page numbers on every footer?

  ○ Is there enough "proof" provided about what you are saying? Metrics, numbers, values?

  ○ Is it something I can forward to other members of the interviewing committee or to my boss?

  ○ Is it too light on content OR too dense with too many unnecessary words?

CHAPTER 16

COVER LETTER OVERHAUL—
A NEW CUT THE CRAP COVER LETTER

Robert and Jessica applied for the same position. Both were qualified based on their résumés and both had an equally fair shot at the job.

Robert included a general cover letter that he used repeatedly to apply for every job opening he looked at. Jessica found out the hiring manager's name and addressed him directly with her **Candidate Packet**. She researched the company and learned about its competition, goals, and products. She also studied the job description and clearly outlined why she was an excellent match for that particular opening (**JD Profile**).

Although the candidates were equally qualified, Jessica's extra effort landed her a job interview. Robert never got called.

Amazingly, most job seekers today, even those with decades of work experience, don't bother sending a cover letter with their résumé. Jonathan typed up a two-sentence email that said "here's my résumé," while Sandy simply left the body of the email blank and attached her résumé with a subject header "Applying." There is no gray area here. Job seekers *must* include a well-written, professionally formatted cover letter with every résumé.

Yes, there are some application websites that force you to just provide a résumé or the contents of your résumé, but read on for tricks and mistakes.

IF a candidate provides a cover letter, they are often poorly written and selfish. By selfish, I mean they use the word "I" repeatedly, regurgitating the same résumé information, and they look like a template the candidate sends to any job. So, *Cut the Crap* and overhaul your cover letter!

The purpose of a cover letter in today's highly competitive era is to...

- ...grab attention and entice the recipient to strongly consider you as a candidate .
- ...concisely send key messages as a quick at-a-glance.
- ...punch the reasons why you are the BEST candidate for their job.

A cover letter should **not**...

- ...repeat the information in your résumé.
- ...share your career goal that has nothing to do with the position you are writing about.
- ...just inform that your résumé is attached. Immediately stop using *"Please accept this application in response to..."*

SOLUTION: THE NEW CUT THE CRAP COVER LETTER

The new Cut the Crap Cover Letter will make you stand out in the crowded applicant market because you will clearly define why you are the BEST candidate for THEIR job, based on THEIR job description.

NOTE: The *only way* you can write this new cover letter is to complete Chapter 15.

Your cover letter will explain what you can do for your "buyer," not what you are selling. Your mission is to give the reader the best peek at your background, which encourages them to want to learn more by reading your résumé. Catch yourself doing an "old" cover letter, which jams all of your selling features into one blob, hoping they find a few morsels.

Your new cover letter has 3 Sections: P.R.R. = Purpose, Reasons, Request

A. Opening: **Purpose** and relevance of this communication or application

B. Body: Top 3 **Reasons** why you are the BEST candidate for this specific position

C. Closing: **Request**, asking for the position and next step (call to action)

Once you do one new cover letter, you will find them so easy and your best preparation for the interview you so badly want.

NEW: Your overhauled and now-impactful cover letter will be sent twice. First: It is the body of your email. Second: It is the first page of your attachment in your CTC Candidate Packet. See Chapter 15 if you skipped it.

NOTE: Read Chapter 13 "Email Etiquette," as all of those rules, tricks, and mistakes apply here.

TRICKS

1 If someone referred you to the position, put that in the first sentence of your cover letter. *"Sally McCay at <company> referred me to this position since we worked together four years ago."*

2 If you were not given the recipient's name officially, then use the first sentence to explain how you found them. *"I found you on LinkedIn and am hopeful that you can either assist me or direct this correspondence to the hiring manager."*

3 Keep the cover letter short and easy to read. Don't make the reader have to scroll through a lot of e-mail. Send it to yourself first and see if it shows on your PC screen without having to page down.

4 Bullet points are great for the body.

5 Use the same font as your résumé. You can even use the same header that you use in your résumé with your name and contact information. Assure your contact information is complete, either in the header or the signature block.

6 Feel free to consider one or two additional sentences that enhance your message. An example: *"What you won't see on my résumé is my passion for sales in addition to marketing. The two need to work hand in hand."* Or *"My analytical skills and attention to detail will enable me to help solve your challenging problems and ensure a high-quality output."*

7 Have a great subject head. If you are applying speculatively, state the type of role you are ideally seeking. "*Sales Manager seeks Business Development position.*"

8 Save a "Cover Letter Checklist" that you refer to prior to pressing "send" on every cover letter:

✓ The contact name and company name are correct.

✓ Letter mentions the position you are applying for.

✓ Your personal information (name, address, home phone, cellphone, email) is all included and correct.

✓ If you have a contact at the company, you have mentioned him or her in the first sentence.

✓ Font is 10 or 12 pt. and easy to read (Calibri or Arial, for example) and matches the font in your résumé.

✓ There are no spelling, grammatical, or typographical errors. You have read it out loud.

✓ You have kept a copy for your records.

 MISTAKES

NOTE: See all of the Mistakes in Chapter 13. In addition to those, the following are cover letter specific:

Mistake #1: Regurgitating your résumé. 9 out of 10 cover letters do this. It is uninspiring and adds zero value.

Mistake #2: Starting almost every sentence with "I." Huge turn-off for the reader and unnecessary.

Mistake #3: Generic cover letter. The recipient can tell immediately.

Mistake #4: Wordy, tiny font.

Mistake #5: Forgetting the attachment: If you are sending a cover letter, you are obviously also sending a résumé or CV (CV is short for Curriculum Vitae, which is just a fancy word for résumé) or application form as an attachment. Many candidates forget the attachment and then have to send another email correcting this. We all make this error from time to time. Just try not to do it on the most important activity of your life... securing your next job. The new Microsoft Office 2013 and Office 365 have a new feature in Outlook, an "attachment reminder" with a prompt that says, "You may have forgotten to attach a file." Very helpful.

 EXCUSES

Excuse #1: *"Hiring managers don't read cover letters anymore."* You should always assume your résumé will merit a look at your cover letter and vice versa. Always include one and make it exceptional so you stand out from the crowd. What if all of the other candidates did a cover letter and your application came in without? What is the downside? If a hiring manager wants to flip to the résumé, they will.

Excuse #2: *"There is no job description or the job description is not very clear."* You still need to do a cover letter. Search for identical or similar jobs in other companies or on job boards, ask your network what they think the skills and qualifications might be, and do the best job you can. The good news is that all candidates for that job are on the same level playing field. So you will still shine with your best effort. Focus on the top skills that you believe that hiring manager will need. An example of today's most important skills for business people in general are: interpersonal teamwork, verbal communications, written communications, analytical, computer skills, and leadership.

Excuse #3: *"I have been unemployed for a long period of time"* or *"I am making a major career change."* Emphasize your strongest qualifications. Focus on what you *can* contribute and how your skills will benefit the employer. Address relevant skills, abilities, education, and experience that demonstrate you will do high-quality work. Do not add extraneous information about your unemployment. Yes, they may ask about it during the interview or phone screen and you will be prepared to answer it there. See Chapters 9 and 17 on interviews. IF you feel compelled to add something to your cover letter, here is a sample: *"In March, 2012, ABC Company experienced a significant workforce reduction and my position was eliminated. Since then, I have remained active in the American Marketing Association and completed online courses in statistics, advanced Excel, and branding."*

HOMEWORK ASSIGNMENT: HOW TO WRITE THE NEW CTC COVER LETTER

Step 1: Place the **job description** and your new **CTC JD Profile** on the table in front of you. See the prior chapter and download the tools at **http://DanaManciagli.com/book-tools**.

Step 2: If you have a network contact who knows this position and hiring manager, ask her what the **3 most important qualifications** are for this position. If you don't know anybody, make your best judgment call and write a #1, #2, and #3 on your **CTC JD Profile**, indicating the stack rank order of the 3 most important criteria the hiring manager is going to judge candidates on.

Step 3: Write the cover letter. It is okay to have a more standardized opening and closing, but the body is dramatically different for each position. Remember: P.R.R. = Purpose, Reasons, Request

A. Opening Samples: **Purpose** and relevance of this communication or application

- ◆ *"I would like to express my deep interest in the <Marketing Manager> position <####> at the <Baywood Corporation>."*

- ◆ *"The <Baywood Corporation's> <Marketing Manager> position <####> seems very important and intriguing and I am excited to apply."*

- ◆ Second Sentence: *"I learned about the position opening on your company's career website"* OR *"<Name> referred me to you and felt I would be a good fit for your need."*

B. Body Samples: Top 3 **Reasons** why you are the BEST candidate for this specific position

- ◆ "After comparing your job description with my background, and doing further research on your business, the following are the three main reasons why I believe I am a highly qualified candidate:

   1. You are looking for <8-10> years in technology testing and I have 11 years, both at <company> and <company>.

   2. <Baywood Corporation> needs someone with skills in teamwork and cross-group collaboration

and I led a cross-function team at <company> with a <$> revenue target.

3. The Marketing Manager position will be managing 3 people and I have 7 years managing teams ranging from 3 to 22 with positive feedback on my management style."

♦ Alternatively, tables can be very useful in the body of the cover letter:

After comparing your job description with my background and doing further research on your business, the following are the three main reasons why I believe I am a highly qualified candidate.

Marketing Manager Position ####	John Howard's Qualifications
8-10 years technology testing	11 years at <company> and <company> with <any statistics about good performance>
Strong proven skills in teamwork and cross-group collaboration	Led a multi-function and multi-geography team at <company> with a <$> incremental revenue target. We exceeded the target by 8%.
Managerial responsibility for 3 people	7 years managing team sizes of 3 to 22 with positive feedback on my management style.

Note: if you do a table, a nice touch is to remove the lines or select a nice design from the Office ribbon under table tools/design.

C. Closing Samples: **Request**—asking for the position and next step (call to action)

♦ *"Mr. Johnson, I am not only a fit for your position, but I am passionate about your industry and <marketing> function. May I please request a phone and/or face-to-face interview? If I don't hear back from you or a member of your organization,*

I will follow up with you on <Day, Date, Time>. (5 working days from the day this cover letter lands.)

Thank you for your time and consideration,

<full signature block> (See email etiquette in Chapter 13)

Attachment: Candidate Packet for John Howard for Position ####

COVER LETTER TEMPLATE:

<<Your page margins should be no smaller than 1 inch. Your font should match your résumé and be 11 or 12 pt.>>

Dear Mr. /Ms. _____ *<<Use the name or Director of Human Resources.>>* Date

<<Hit "enter" 2 times after date and then include the following information>>

I would like to express my deep interest in the <Marketing Manager> position <####> at the <Baywood Corporation>. <Name> referred me to you and felt I would be a good fit for your need.

<<Hit "enter" 2 times>>

After comparing your job description with my background and doing further research on your business, the following are the three main reasons why I believe I am a highly qualified candidate

Marketing Manager Position ####	<John Howard's> Qualifications
8-10 years technology testing	11 years at <company> and <company> with <any statistics about good performance>.
Strong proven skills in teamwork and cross-group collaboration	Led a multi-function and multi-geography team at <company> with a <$> incremental revenue target. We exceeded the target by 8%.
Managerial responsibility for 3 people	7 years managing team sizes of 3 to 22 with positive feedback on my management style.

<<Hit "enter" 2 times>>

"Mr. Johnson, I am not only a fit for your position, but I am passionate about your industry and <marketing> function. May I please request a phone and/or face-to-face interview? If I don't hear back from you or a member of your organization, I will follow up with you on <Day, Date, Time>.

<<Hit "enter" 2 times>>

Thank you for your time and consideration,

<<Hit "enter" 2 times>>

John Howard <Your typed name, first and last>

Your email

Your preferred phone (don't put home phone unless you answer it!)

Your full street address

Your LinkedIn address (learn how to make hyperlinks so the recipient can just click)

<<Hit "enter" 2 times>>

Attachment: John Howard's Candidate Package

CHAPTER 17
WINNING INTERVIEWS TO WIN A JOB

In Chapter 9, I coached you how to "pre-prepare" for every interview, even before you apply to your first job opportunity. Now, I want to help you WIN the job as a result of a job-specific interview. So we have fast-forwarded through time. You are prepared, you have been applying using brand new techniques, and you earned an interview. Congratulations! Regardless if the interview medium is phone, web video, or face to face, an interview requires an intense focus on how you sound, how you look, how you behave, non-verbal gestures, and so much more.

Learning how to interview reminds me of learning how to swing a golf club. There are so many things to learn and practice, ranging from my grip to the way I take the club back, pivot, swing, and follow through. Any slight error in one step can cause that little 1.7-inch-diameter white ball to go anywhere but straight. Interviewing is the same.

There are thousands of websites and guidance on "how to interview for a job." Instead of repeating all of that here, my goal is to highlight how to be THE BEST in today's new era of job search. The hiring and recruiting process has changed since the last time you interviewed, and my goal is to help you increase your odds of winning the job as a result of your great interview. A "good" interview is no longer good enough.

4 Principles of Job Interviews. Once you embrace these, you are on your way to success.

1. **The Interviewer has an agenda.** Know their agenda. During the interview process, there are three main questions that need to be answered to help the HR person, hiring manager, or interviewer determine if you're the right fit for the job:

    o   Can this person do the job?

    o   Will he/she do the job?

    o   Will he/she fit in with the company culture?

2. **The interview is all about THEM**, the company, the hiring manager, the interviewer. News flash: It's not about YOU sharing all you can about YOU. Everything you say and do must be relevant and meaningful to THEM. Be very careful.

3. **The interview is your performance of a lifetime.** You are being watched with every step you take, every move you make, including how you look. Think about it. From a company perspective, this is your BEST day. You have your best outfit on, you have been able to prepare with research, you can say amazing things about yourself and even brag a little. Once the company hires you, it's potentially downhill from your best day. The point is that if you can't be a great listener or communicator on this day, OR if you make huge errors such as bad-mouthing a prior boss, then you probably won't win this job.

    Don't be fooled by venue, either. In this new era of job search, you may be meeting in a Starbucks café or on a web conference. Or the meeting might be called an "informational" or information-gathering meeting, which is an interview in disguise. Alternatively, the meeting might be with a friend of a friend who might have the job you are looking for. Safest bet: If there is a job in the midst, put that interview guard UP (avoiding mistakes) and keep it UP.

4. **You can't over-prepare for an interview.** In my 30+ years of hiring, interviewing, and recruiting for other teams and coaching, I have NEVER heard a hiring manager say, "Wow, that candidate was too prepared for my interview," or, "No way, she was too organized and had answers to every question I asked." So I'm going to assume you have read Chapter 9 prior to reading on with this chapter. I won't be repeating that guidance here.

SOLUTION

❏ **Bring the Right Stuff:** Save this as a checklist before every interview. I guarantee that the day you don't check your checklist, you will forget something important.

✓ Portfolio or pad holder with plenty of paper and two pens

✓ Multiple copies of your résumé

✓ A copy of the job description with any notes on it that you want to ask about

✓ Multiple copies of your complete **CTC Candidate Packet** with your **cover letter, CTC JD Profile,** and résumé, all stapled together (Chapter 15)

✓ Multiple copies of your list of references (although this is rarely requested during an interview)

✓ Work samples (if relevant). This should never be proprietary information, so check with your prior employer.

✓ Breath mints (before you enter the building and in between interviews)

✓ Small bottle of water, protein bar, or snack

✓ Briefcase to hold all of the above. For ladies, it can be a larger purse. Avoid walking in with your arms full, unable to shake hands, or looking disorganized.

What **not** to bring to an interview:

○ Cellphone

○ Music player

○ Gum

○ Cigarettes

○ Candy

○ Soda or coffee

○ Laptop or tablet, not even to take notes with, unless it is requested

❒ **Look and Sound the Part:**

Interview Attire. Dressing formally and appropriately sends a signal to the interviewer that you cared enough to want to make a good first impression. Inversely, not being dressed appropriately will hurt you.

Job search is all about first impressions. You want your appearance to convey a confident, respectful, professional, and prepared job seeker. Remember, you are "on stage"... and this interview day is your BEST day. Obviously, you want the interviewer to concentrate on your skills, qualifications, and fit with their job description specifications.

However, if you look disheveled or too casual, you may be remembered for the wrong reasons. Interviewers know that what you wear is not your normal day-to-day attire, and it may not even be the everyday style of their office. Be sure you understand the product or service of the company. Applying for a position with a law firm requires a different "attitude" in dressing than for an internet company or manufacturing facility. However, during my 30 years as a hiring manager and candidate, I have never heard an interviewer complain that "they came in dressed too nicely."

The following are 13 mistakes that may derail your ability to make a professional first impression and may undermine your ability to WIN that job.

For Men:

- Men's Suits

    Mistake #1: Wearing a suit with bold colors, large prints, stripes, plaids, or funky patterns.

    Correction: Wear a jacket in a dark, solid color, such as navy or charcoal/gray.

    Mistake #2: Wearing a suit jacket with pants that don't match.

    Correction: If you wear a two-piece suit, be sure it matches or wear a blazer and slacks—no jeans!

    Mistake #3: Wearing a suit made of an exotic fabric, such as suede, leather, or velvet.

    Correction: Wear a jacket of neutral fibers (depending on the season), like wool, a wool blend, cotton, or linen.

    Mistake #4: Wearing a garment that doesn't fit.

Correction: Anything too large or too small is a dead giveaway that it is not yours! Invest in ONE "interview" outfit; it's worth it!

Men's Socks and Footwear:

Mistake #5: Wearing no socks, short socks, or socks with large prints, patterns, or bright colors.

Correction: Wear socks mid-calf-length so no skin is visible when you sit down. Generally, your socks should match the bottom of your slacks.

Mistake #6: Wearing dress boots, athletic shoes, deck shoes, crocs, sandals, or flip flops.

Correction: Wear leather shoes with or without laces; dressy loafers are okay for a casual facility—shinier materials, such as patent leather, are too dressy.

Mistake #7: Wearing a short-sleeve shirt, collarless shirt, ill-fitting shirt, rolled up sleeves, or wrinkled shirt.

Correction: Wear a well-pressed, long-sleeve, button-down-the-front shirt with a collar. The shirt should fit your neck perfectly (if it is too tight, it will look strained, and if neckline is too large, your tie will drag the collar shirt down). Here's the trick: Hang your shirt in or around a steamy shower for about 5 minutes to get the wrinkles out.

Mistake #8: Wearing bold shirts in flashy colors or prints.

Correction: Choose a solid or conservatively striped shirt.

♦ Men's Ties:

Mistake #9: Wearing a flashy tie, a tie with religious, political, or sports symbols, or with cartoon characters.

Correction: Wear a tie with neat repeating patterns or a traditionally striped tie. When in doubt, be on the conservative side.

♦ Men's Jewelry:

Mistake #10: Wearing excessive amounts of jewelry or body jewelry (ear, eyebrow, nose rings, etc.).

Correction: Limit yourself to a watch and one ring per hand.

For Women: While many of the mistakes and appropriate recommendations above apply to women as well, there are a couple of additional points for women:

♦ Suit: Wear a pant suit or a knee-length skirt suit.

♦ Hosiery: When wearing a skirt suit, wear neutral or flesh-tone stockings. In spite of the no-hosiery trend, this interview needs to be your BEST day, so err on the formal side.

♦ Shoes: Wear a low-heel shoe versus flats or four-or-more-inch high heels. No sandals, tennis shoes, or flip flops. Depending on the season, boots are okay too.

♦ Necklines: Too low a neckline can give the interviewer the wrong impression. Button up your blouses. Do not show any undergarment shoulder straps.

♦ Hemlines: Wear a suit that reaches the middle of the knee or 1-2 inches below the knee. When legs are crossed, the interviewer may be given the wrong impression.

♦ Perfumes: Do not wear any. Some interviewers may be allergic and you don't want to leave an impression of your perfume in their office all day. Additionally, aromas are very subjective; the interviewer may just not like your scent...ever.

All Genders: Briefcase/Portfolio/Pen:

Mistake #11: Not having anything with you to take notes with. Not having copies of your résumé.

Correction: Bring in a portfolio or briefcase with a clean pad and pens (have backup!), multiple copies of your résumé, notes you have taken to prepare for the interview, including questions you will ask them, and a copy of the job description. Toss in a bottle of water and a nutritional bar in case you are waiting or are given a short break.

All Genders: Cellphone:

Mistake #12: Talking or texting on your way into the interview area—or worse yet, taking a call during the interview. Your cellphone should be off once you are on the premises.

Correction: Turn off your cellphone as soon as you step out of your vehicle or transportation. Trick: Put a big yellow sticky note on your portfolio to remember.

All Genders: Hats or Sunglasses:

Mistake #13: Wearing a hat or sunglasses in the building for your meeting.

Correction: Do not wear a hat and remove sunglasses immediately upon entering the building. (No sunglasses up on top of your head—remove them completely.)

These recommendations are for the traditional, conservative industries. If you are pursuing a position in the creative or artistic field, you may need to adjust these recommendations. However, always err on the conservative side of the industry unless you feel you simply could not be happy working in a somewhat conservative environment.

Remember, this is your BEST day and you want to be remembered for your "total package," including the presentation of your skills and capabilities. Yes, dressing for success is important. As Shakespeare said, *"All the world is a stage and we are merely players."* The interview is your "stage."

o **Be clean, odor-free.** If you come to an interview smelling of cigarette smoke or bad breath, you will already have one strike against you. Too much perfume or not enough deodorant are common mistakes.

o **Grooming** is important, as well, so invest in a haircut and manicure (men and women!). Shine those shoes while you're at it.

o **Handshake.** Your handshake should be firm—not sticky or wimpy. To avoid sweaty palms, visit the restroom, wash your hands, and then run them under cool water prior to the interview. Dry your hands well, as nobody wants to shake a wet hand, even if it's water. Keep your palms open rather than clenched in a fist and keep a tissue you in your pocket to (surreptitiously) wipe them.

- **Sound professional:** Be polite and keep an even tone to your speech. Don't be too loud or too quiet. Remember your manners and thank the interviewer for taking the time to meet with you. Don't use slang. Speak clearly and confidently. Be humble as well.

❒ **Non-Verbal Success:** The evaluation of your non-verbal communication will start as soon as you walk into the company's lobby and continue until the interview is finished. If your non-verbal communication skills aren't up to par, it won't matter how well you answer the questions.

- Be *happy*: Hiring managers want to hire happy people. Only say positive things, even if you have a less-than-positive experience in the past. Keep your emotions to yourself and do not show anger or frown. Smile!

- Be *present*: Sit up, give a solid handshake, and make eye contact. Leaning back in your seat with your legs crossed at the knee sends a message you are too relaxed for an interview setting.

- Be *energetic*: Lean forward a little towards the interviewer so you appear interested and engaged. However, keep your feet on the floor and your lower back against the back of the chair so you don't look like you are lunging forward.

- *Listen Attentively.* When you sit down, put your portfolio on their desk to take notes, yet don't take up too much of their space. Open up to a blank page with a pen ready. Don't interrupt. Ever. Let them finish their full thought then pause another few seconds. Don't jump on their last word with your message.

- *Be calm*: Yeah, right. You're as nervous as a cat in a room filled with rocking chairs and you need to relax? Try. Breathe. Smile. Not sure what to do with your hands? Hold a pen and your notepad or rest an arm on the chair or on your lap so you look comfortable. Don't let your arms fly around the room when you're making a point. Light hand gestures are good.

☐ **Know the Job:**

- Most candidates do not *study the job description*. The hiring manager took time to describe, as best as possible, what the job description (JD) is. While it will never answer all questions you have and some JDs are better written than others, it is the best tool you have to be successful in an interview. Peel it apart, line by line, and research what the terms mean if you don't know.

- Develop a Job Description Profile for each opportunity. Compare your skills and background to the job description. See Chapter 15 for the template on how to do this well, called the "Cut the Crap (CTC) JD Profile."

☐ **Know Yourself:**

- Beyond standard strengths and weaknesses, are you well-versed and have written notes about YOU? Do you know the day-to-day duties where you are very skilled and skills you need to develop?

- Do you know why you want this particular position? What are you interested in this particular industry? Why are you interested in this company?

- What have other managers or peers said about your work style, leadership style, or management style in the past? Have you reviewed prior reviews or feedback tools? Have you taken any work style assessments such as the Myers-Briggs Type Indicator?

☐ **Ask for the Job at the End:** Managers want to hire people who really want the position. Most candidates don't say that. Say it in writing and at the interview. *"Joanne, I want to share how passionate I am for this position and there are three main reasons: It's fast-paced, I have experience with these partners in the past, and I can learn so much from you and others."*

Another good close is, *"What is the next step?"* or, *"When do you plan to make a decision?"*

Finally, ask them for their email address so you can follow up with a thank you note.

 TRICKS

1 See the tricks in Chapter 9.

2 Day before the interview: Prepare for the interview logistics. Lay out your clothing, set your alarm clock, be sure you know where you are going, check your car for gas, make copies of documents, organize your portfolio and briefcase or purse, etc.

3 Day before the interview: Prepare for the interview questions. Even if you have been to interviews in the past month, re-read your 3 bullet points per interview question. Review the questions you will be asking them as well.

4 Night before the interview: Go back to the company's website and read their latest announcements, press releases, speeches, and people changes.

5 *"The Law of 3s:"* For every question, both during your preparation AND during your interview, state no more than 3 things then *stop talking*. A full stop, not just a pause for breath. If the interviewer wants more, she will ask. If the silence becomes too awkward, you can ask, "Would you like more information?"

6 You will have a pen and paper open on the table during a face-to-face interview. In the far right or left margin, you can have some short clues to some key interview questions and answers that you are nervous about remembering.

7 When a question is asked, feel free to write some words about the question down so you can peek at it and stay on track.

8 Pause after the question is asked and think. Feel free to scribble 3 words down that will be your 3 points.

9 Smile and breathe. Feel free to take a sip of water.

10 **Humility** is treasured. Find an opportunity to say, *"I have not developed that skill, but I'm very eager to learn,"* or, *"It's a new skill for me, so I consider myself a novice and I'm excited to get to the advanced level."* Another great way to show humility is to ask them a question back, either instead of answering or right after you answer. Let's say they ask you if know the NMFP Organization. *"No, I have not learned that industry term or I don't know that organization. Can you tell me about it?"*

11 **Phone interviews**: Wear a nice top in case the interviewer wants to do a video interview using Skype or some other technology.

MISTAKES

Mistake #1: Insensitivity to the company's brand or products. Candidates have set a competitor's technology down on the table of a technology interview (and proceeded to sing its praises). While it won't get you thrown out, your judgment on your BEST day was flawed.

Mistake #2: Being too honest. Many interviewers have a friendly style, both in person and on the phone. They make small talk, try to make you feel at ease, even laugh about something. However, as a result, many candidates let their "interview performance" guard down. Some signs: *"Between you and me…"* or *"Well, the truth is, my prior manager was an idiot."*

You're nervous. You want to be their buddy. But the interviewer has only one objective, and that objective is at the beginning of this chapter:

- Can this person do the job?
- Will he/she do the job?
- Will he/she fit in with the company culture?

They're not looking for a buddy.

Mistake #3: Being negative. Bashing a current or prior company's management, products, vision, etc. How many times did our parents teach us the golden rule of *"if you don't have anything nice to say, don't say anything at all?"*

Mistake #4: Offering unsolicited information that hurts your candidacy. Some recent examples include, *"I need to drop off my baby at 9:00 a.m. and pick her up at 3:00 p.m. Do you have* *flexible hours?"* Or a recent candidate for a finance position asked, *"I need to brush up on my Excel skills. Will you guys reimburse me for a class?"*

Mistake #5: Lying. This includes embellishing, exaggerating, misleading, taking credit for something you didn't do, etc.

Mistake #6: Cocky, not being self-aware. Interview scenario: "What are your weaknesses?" The candidate replies *"Hmmmm...I have really been perfecting my style, so I don't have any big ones."* That person is still looking for a job right now.

Interview scenario: "Can you tell me about an experience where you launched a new product?"

(Now, we all know that 70-80% of new products fail). "Yes, I launched 8 major products in the last 7 years and they're all big winners now."

Interviewer: "Can you highlight one that didn't go as well as the others?" *"That's hard. They were all hugely successful based on my leadership and ability to design a great marketing plan and lead my team to victory."*

Mistake #7: Forgetting to ask for the job, about the next steps, or "going for the close." Not appearing eager, interested, or hungry. *"Thank you, bye." "I appreciate your time, Mr. Jones."*

No! In every interview, even if you have five in a row, and regardless who you are meeting with:

- *"Mr. <name>, do you think I have the skills and passion to be your top candidate?"*

- *"Realizing you may have more candidates to see, am I a strong or top candidate for your <X> position?"*

- *"I would very much like to secure this position. What are the next steps?"*

Mistake #8: Did not do any research on the company, industry, position, and people. Many candidates say they don't have time to visit the company website, haven't searched the interviewer's background, or don't know what the division or department does (and it's widely available). If they have done research, there is no demonstration of any note-taking from the research, or they haven't read the job description in great detail, on and on.

Mistake #9: No copy of your résumé or cover letter.

- *"Oh, it was in the email I sent you, so I thought you would print it." "The recruiter said you had it." "I just gave out my last one." "I have it here on my laptop...I can turn it on and show it to you."*

- Always, always bring your résumé, cover letter, and any other documents you want to share.

Mistake #10: Asking about salary in an interview. Never ever, ever, ever raise the "money" subject. Your mission is to get the offer. A dialogue and possible negotiation will follow. There are websites that help with salary ranges so you can go in educated, but do not ask.

Mistake #11: Not listening to the question. Most of them are quite easy...if you listen.

Mistake #12: Not having interesting questions.

Mistake #13: Talking too much, rambling, taking too much time, random thoughts.

Mistake #14: Not taking notes. An interview is a dialogue as well as a performance. The person on the other end of the table or phone is giving clues, tips, and information along the way that will all be valuable to you for future interviews or on the job. Write EVERYTHING down.

EXCUSES

Because interviews are the most critical decision-making actions for both you and the employer, I am going to repeat the excuses from the interview preparation Chapter 9, and add others.

Excuse #1: *"It's just a phone screen by HR or a recruiter."* You need as much preparation for this as you do a formal interview. If you bomb here, you don't move to the next phase. You will also gain some insights about the position and company AND they will ask you if you have any questions for them.

Excuse #2: *"It's a phone interview, not a face-to-face, so it must not be that important."* First, this thinking is flawed. Second, you get to have notes in front of you! You should be amazingly prepared, as you don't have to memorize anything. See Chapter 12 for phone etiquette tips.

Excuse #3: *"I think the interviewer will frown upon me having notes in front of me."* Get over that. They are still your thoughts, your feedback to the questions, and your interview! Choose one: Option A, you don't get the job because you fumbled through the interview questions (nerves, you forgot some key points), or Option B, you got the job since you showed such interest, preparation, and passion for the position.

Excuse #4: I call this one *"my dog ate my homework."* For over 30 years, asking candidates why they feel they didn't have a good interview, the most common excuses are, *"I had a lot going on, personally,"* *"The interviewer was tough,"* *"I got lost, was late, so I was flustered,"* *"They didn't tell me it was going to be a 'real' interview,"* *"I thought it was just an informational for me to get clarity...but it turned into an interview,"* and, *"I* *was sick.*" If you have heard the expression "rise to the occasion," it means meet the challenge, meet expectations in a tough situation, and overcome unexpected circumstances. Remember, your interview is your BEST DAY. And the definition of an "interview" is any contact with anybody who can help you win a job in this very competitive job search market. This means it can be a cup of coffee with a network contact, a phone screen, an email, an informational meeting, or a formal interview.

 ## HOMEWORK ASSIGNMENT

☐ #1 Complete the full homework in Chapter 9.

☐ #2 Refresh your answers based on this specific job interview you are preparing for.

☐ #3 Write down the 5-10 questions YOU will ask the interviewer(s). They may be the same in Chapter 9, but you may add a few that are specific to the job description, the position, or the company/division.

☐ #4 Prepare your interview attire and items you will bring with you.

CHAPTER 18
THANK YOU AND FOLLOW-UP

The weakest part of the job search process is the deplorable state of follow-up. It's so much more than thank you notes, but those aren't even being sent. Job seekers, thank you and follow-up communications are not optional; they are required.

Here are the benefits of great follow-up, all of which can put you ahead of another candidate:

1. Shows persistence.

2. Allows you to expand, reinforce, or clarify something discussed in the interview.

3. Good manners are always valued.

4. Prevents them from forgetting about you.

5. Reinforces that you want the job.

Here are the downsides of NOT following up:

- A portion of hiring managers will dismiss an applicant who does not send a post-interview thank you note, saying it indicates poor follow-through and a lack of interest in the position.

- Other candidates will follow up, so you lost an opportunity to compete for that job.

If you mastered Chapter 17, then your follow-up began in the interview when you asked, *"What is the next step?"* or, *"When do you plan to make a decision?"* With that knowledge, you can time your follow-up post-interview.

 SOLUTION

World-class follow-up looks like:

- Sending a note within 24-48 hours while it's still fresh in your mind—and the company's.
- Addressing a note to each individual person you met with.
- Spelling everyone's name correctly, including the company's.

Sample flow of a thank you note:

- Start by thanking them for the opportunity to meet and acknowledge that they took time out of their day to do so.
- Next, note why you think you'd be a good fit for the role. No more than 3 reasons. Bullet points are optimal as well. This is an opportunity to elaborate on why you are a great fit, in writing, beyond your initial cover letter and interview.
- In close, hit 3 points: 1.) Express your interest; 2.) Commit to following up with them again within a specified timeframe; and 3.) Thank them, again, for their time and consideration.

Sample ideas of follow-up after the thank you note:

- Begin with a pleasantry, followed by a sentence explaining where you left off during your last communication. *"You had* *indicated to me that you'd be making your final decision during the week of <date >, and I just wanted to follow up to see where you are in that decision."*

- Include something of value in your follow-up instead of being perceived as nagging. Perhaps you just completed some training, closed a big deal, or finished a major project. If you are volunteering or taking outside courses while unemployed, talk about that.

- Close with the next follow-up you will initiate. Don't ask them to call you back. Instead, let them know that *"I'll follow up again within a few days, but in case you need to reach me, here is the best contact number: xxx-xxx-xxxx."*

TRICKS

1 Always appear gracious, positive, patient, and interested. Speak in a very respectful manner if you're leaving a voice-mail message, acknowledging that *"I know you are very busy, but I wanted to follow up on the email I sent you and that I'm still very interested in the position."*

2 When following up with an email, always attach the prior email you are referring to. If there was an attachment to the prior email, reattach it, as appropriate.

3 Match the communication medium the interviewer has been using, i.e. returning emails with emails, phone calls with phone calls.

MISTAKES

Mistake #1: Scathing follow up emails from job seekers who think they're out of the running.

Mistake #2: Rudeness or impatience. If the hiring manager gave you a specific date or timeframe, give them some room. Hiring processes take time and you don't want to seem overly anxious.

Mistake #3: One-line emails: *"Can you call me back?"*

Mistake #4: Group thank you notes—implies a little laziness and is not personal.

Mistake #5: In a personal thank you note, your copy and paste didn't work so it was addressed *"Dear Sally"* and at the end it said *"Thank you, again, Bob."*

Mistake #6: Misspellings, grammar, punctuation errors. This is another writing sample for the employer!

Mistake #7: Gimmicks. Do not send flowers, a gift, nothing.

Mistake #8: Do not have a friend "swing by" the hiring manager's office and ask, *"How is Bob doing for your position hiring. Isn't he great?"*

EXCUSES

Excuse #1: *"I knocked the interview out of the park, so no need to send anything since I'll get the job."* Well, aside from being too confident (cocky), which could have hurt you in the interview, there is no excuse for not being polite. And what if you were good in the interview, but not great, and the next candidate did send a compelling note?

Excuse #2: *"I don't have their email address."* Lesson learned. Ask for all email addresses while you are interviewing. However, if you forgot, contact the recruiter, HR manager, or anybody who might be able to give it to you. Simply say, "I would like to send them a thank you note," so your intention is clear.

Excuse #3: *"Thank you notes seem so phony. I'm not the thank you note type."* First, they should be sincere. Sheer appreciation for their time and for considering you as a candidate should be reason enough to take 5 minutes to review your notes from that meeting and craft a thank you note. Second, if you are not the "thank you note type," then learn to be one now!

Excuse #4: *"They told me I will not be the final choice for the position, so no need to thank them."* Wrong. You want to add your interviewers to your network and you may want to contact them again. In addition, what if that company has another position that opens up? Take the high road and always, always send a thank you note and stay in touch after that. In your thank you note, you may say, *"If another position opens up within your organization, I am interested in being considered."*

HOMEWORK ASSIGNMENT

☐ **#1**: Write a template thank you note and follow-up note based on the above guidance and by collecting many samples available online. Save them in your well-organized file for this job search effort (see Chapter 5).

☐ **#2**: Review your samples with at least one person and get their feedback.

☐ **#3**: In your Cut the Crap (CTC) Job Tracker from Chapter 5, be sure you note every time you need to send a thank you note and place that reminder in your Outlook Calendar or other calendar technology.

ABOUT THE AUTHOR

Dana Manciagli has been a corporate executive for more than 30 years and has leveraged her employee hiring and management experience into that of author, blogger, keynote speaker, career coach, and global career expert. Dana has had a remarkable career in global sales and marketing roles in Fortune 500 corporations. Having just recently been a worldwide sales general manager at Microsoft for a decade, Dana previously worked for Kodak as VP of worldwide marketing and climbed the corporate career ladder through Sea-Land, Avery Dennison, and IBM. She also helped grow a technology start-up from early stage to IPO and sale of the company.

Dana has coached, interviewed, and hired thousands of job seekers. As a result, she has developed a proprietary job search and networking process. She has presented her concept at hundreds of career-centric and corporate events and is a prolific writer on the subject. Her ideas and techniques are proven to be as effective for college graduates as for senior executives. She was named a top "Women of Influence" in Seattle, where she lives with her partner, Mathis, and is on the Worldwide Board of Junior Achievement. She is also a breast cancer survivor, received her

MBA at the Thunderbird School of Global Management in Arizona, and speaks Spanish. Dana has two grown boys, Shane and Chad, and loves to golf and travel the world.

You can visit Dana's website at www.DanaManciagli.com.

CPSIA information can be obtained at www.ICGtesting.com
Printed in the USA
BVOW08s1819280515

402028BV00011B/339/P